A VERY MUDDY PLACE

Benjamin Franklin Potts, age twenty-one.
Taken three years before, this photograph was a family keepsake during his eleven-month absence.

A Very Muddy Place

WAR STORIES

Stephen Wendell

Peregrine Publishing
Paris

Peregrine Publishing
www.stephenwendell.com

Copyright © 2019 Stephen Wendell
All rights reserved. Published 2019.

First Edition
Paperback

All Potts family photographs courtesy of the Potts family.
Illustration credits appear in their respective captions.

Cover photograph:
Benjamin Franklin Potts, age twenty-one.
Courtesy of the Potts family.
See also frontispiece.

Cover background:
Three map sheets from *La carte de l'état-major*, 1866.

For bonus material, please visit
https://www.stephenwendell.com/avmp/.

ISBN 979-10-96666-40-9

In memoriam
John Wesley Potts

For the family of
Benjamin Franklin Potts

The (unobserved) past, like the future, is indefinite and exists only as a spectrum of possibilities.
—STEPHEN HAWKING & LEONARD MLODINOW,
THE GRAND DESIGN

Contents

War stories are set in italic type.

Illustrations	ix
Preface	xi
Chronology	xv

PART ONE — FROM TENNESSEE TO THE GREAT WAR

1	The Butte of Vauquois	3
2	Benjamin Potts Registers for the Draft	6
3	Military Induction and Entrainment	9
4	Army Training at Camp Gordon	12
	If it moves, salute it	*12*
5	Embarkation, the *Tunisian*, and the Bridge of Ships	15
6	Enterprise, Tennessee	19
7	Rendezvous with the Thirty-Fifth Division	21
	On a train in France	*21*
8	*In Reserve at Saint-Mihiel*	*27*
9	A Soldier's Sentiment	32
10	Special Job for Private Potts	35
	Traveling from camp to camp, often under fire	*38*
11	*Another Wednesday in the War*	*39*
12	A Potts Family Day of Thanks	40
	The captain forbade them from entering	*40*

PART TWO — THE ARGONNE BATTLE

13	Planning the Meuse-Argonne Offensive	49
14	Prelude to Battle	56
15	*Taking Vauquois*	*58*
16	*Fog of War*	*66*

17	Night Attack	74
18	Montrebeau Wood	79
19	Encounter at Creek's Edge	83
	The German soldier reached for his rifle	*83*
20	Charge to Exermont	84
21	Clyde Brake Boards the *Leviathan*	91
22	The Engineers' Line	96
23	Relieved	99

PART THREE   HOMEWARD

24	Roy Albert Buried Alive!	105
	He was near the spot where a shell landed	*105*
25	Nightmare at Sea	109
26	Permission for Leave	116
	Ben had been told that his brother Roy had died	*117*
27	An Unremarkable Day	119
28	Armistice, or A Railcar in the Woods	120
29	Cruel Days in Sampigny	124
30	Godspeed	126
	When Pershing visited	*128*
31	Easter Aboard the *Manchuria*	129
32	Homecoming	132
	He wanted to fight in WWII	*133*
	The dented helmet	*135*

Appendix I	Discharge and Enlistment Record	137
Appendix II	Alternative Scenario	143
Appendix III	The Truman Encounters	146
Annotated Bibliography		149

Illustrations

Benjamin Franklin Potts, age twenty-one	*frontispiece*
From the US and across the Atlantic	xvi
To the western front	xvii
Butte of Vauquois	4
From the 1910 US census	7
Draft registration card	7
Induction and entrainment	11
Barracks at Camp Gordon	13
The *Tunisian*	16
From the *Tunisian*'s passenger list	17
John Wesley Potts	20
American troops headed for the trenches	22
Thirty-Fifth Division order of battle	23
Marching into reserve at Saint-Mihiel	28
Hand-to-hand combat training	37
Partial map sheet: *Bar-le-Duc, Partie N. E.*	43
Map: *Meuse-Argonne Offensive*	47
French General Foch's plan	51
The American sector	52
Thirty-Fifth Division attack formation	53
Thirty-Fifth Division sector	55
Map section: September 26, morning	61
« Aux combattants et aux morts de Vauquois »	65
Map section: September 26, afternoon	69

Map section: September 27	77
Map section: September 28	81
Map section: September 29	85
The *Vaterland*	91
Clyde Brake Potts in uniform	93
Clyde Brake Potts, the *Leviathan*	95
Map section: September 30	97
Marching south	100
Roy Albert Potts, the *Anselm*	106
Map: *30th Division, Somme Offensive*	108
Clyde Brake Potts, the *Agamemnon*	115
Inspection by the Commander-in-Chief	126
From the *Manchuria*'s passenger list	130
Ben and Mae Potts	135
Honorable Discharge	139
Enlistment Record	140

Preface

My great grandfather, like many veterans, didn't talk much about his wartime experience. The family has only his discharge paper and a few war stories told by the man who lived them. His journey began when he was drafted into the US Army in June 1918. He went to France and served with the American Expeditionary Force before returning home in May the next year. A century later, I set out on my own journey to discover more about my ancestor's experience in the war.

I remember Benjamin Franklin Potts, whom my cousins, siblings, and I called "Grandpa" or "Grandpa Ben," from family visits to the red brick house, where he and Granny lived their quiet years in Tennessee Ridge, Tennessee. In his seventies and eighties when I knew him, he walked with a cane but stood straight. He was not a tall man, five feet three in his youth, and now his frame was slight. He wore what I thought of as "old man's pants," wide-legged trousers that hung from the hips, held by suspenders. The trousers were dark, but his shirt—invariably a gift from one of his children or something Granny got for him at the Dollar General Store in Erin—was always colorful. His chin was stubbly, his eyes pale blue. When he grinned, which was often, his ears perked up. He spoke around a plug of tobacco, and his voice wheezed with age, rendering his speech inarticulate to my young ears.

The family sat in lawn chairs arrayed around the carport, out of the hot summer sun. Voices, chatting, echoed between brick and cement. Children wiggled in their chairs, flicking sweat bees from their arms, as they'd been taught, not swatting. Adults sipped Granny's iced tea from plastic cups. A breeze stirred the air, and someone asked about the war.

Tobacco-stained Folgers can beside his chair, cane hooked on its arm, Grandpa obliged with a story or two. I was too young to understand the context, but I heard mentioned faraway places with fantastical and unpronounceable names, like "Lay Voadge," the "Muse," and the "All-gone Forest."

My cousin Bruce Potts listened more attentively than I. He recently sat down with Uncle Jesse, Grandpa Ben's last surviving child, to refresh their memories, to tell the old war stories again, secondhand now that the main character is no longer with us. The stories collected by Bruce and his brother John are the only written memories, that I know of, concerning B. F. Potts in the war.

When I began the journey a hundred years after my great grandfather, I thought it would be easy—recite the anecdotes, give the context, throw in some ambiance.... As I got deeper into the research, though, I discovered more than I could have hoped for.

Although there's a lot of history in those last months of the war, in that short time there are only so many occasions that certain of the anecdotes could have taken place. That I could narrow down the times and places of most of the stories to within a few likely days—and, in some cases, to the day—on my ancestor's journey has been a tremendous reward.

The anecdotes are set off in the text. Other than editing for clarity, I left them as recorded by my cousins.

Scenes narrated in present tense are fictional, giving a dramatic account of certain events as they may have played out. They are meant to provide ambiance and show a possible—if not probable—scenario.

I use imperial units throughout the text, except in discussion of distance in battle. Sources of the period often give distance in metric, and the maps are divided into one-thousand-meter-square grids. To imagine these distances, the reader may substitute yards for meters and arrive at an adequate representation in the mind's eye.

Though the research often allowed me to fill in blanks of the soldier's whereabouts, sometimes not enough information is available, and the author is forced to make conjecture. I hope the text is clear where I speculate or invent details.

Throughout, my goal is to place the anecdotes both on the map and on the timeline. In any instance where the text conflicts with the historical record, I'm wrong.

My thanks to Inez Klein for the mimeograph copy of the discharge paper that put me on the trail. Thanks also to Bruce and John Potts for writing down the stories, to Sharon Potts Webster for helping to decipher faded documents, and to the extended Potts family for their encouragement during the writing of this book.

I owe an enormous debt of gratitude to friends Juliet Green and David Lister, who gave me lodging and good company for several months in the year this book was written. I'll be a lifetime in the debt's repayment, every gesture of which is, for me, an immense pleasure.

When we hear an old soldier's war stories, we might fail to appreciate the momentous occasion. So far away, so long ago, the stories, integral to the teller, are remote to the audience. While the soldier is humble and the soldier's part in events necessarily small, we are well inclined to lend our attention to the words, to remember the places, the names, the details of events. For the stories are a part of history that are unwritten in any book, and though they dwindle with time, memories are rekindled with remembering.

Stephen Wendell
February 7, 2019
Paris, France

Chronology

The table below gives dates and places on B. F. Potts's itinerary with corresponding events. Bold entries are those for which we have either a document with his name on it or an anecdote that coincides with the historical record. Entries in italics are uncertain.

On the accompanying maps, white markers indicate places on the soldier's journey. Black markers show national capitals for reference or places through which his brothers traveled.

DATE	PLACE	EVENT
1917		
April 6	Tennessee Ridge, TN	US enters war
June 5	**Houston County Courthouse, Erin, TN**	**Draft registration**
1918		
June 27	**Houston County Courthouse, Erin, TN**	**Induction**
June 29	Camp Gordon, GA	Training
August 24	Montreal, Canada	Embarkation *Tunisian*
September 8	London, England	Debarkation

Chronology

DATE	PLACE	EVENT
September 8	Newhaven or Southampton, England, to Le Havre, Cherbourg, or Calais, France	Channel crossing
September 11	Nancy	Rendezvous with Thirty-Fifth Division
September 12-15	Haye Forest	Saint-Mihiel battle
September 21-25	Auzéville	Battle preparation
September 26-30	Vauquois to Exermont	Meuse-Argonne Offensive
October 6-11	Vavincourt	Rest camp
October 14–November 6	**Sommedieue Sector, Bouée Subsector**	**In the trenches**
November 10–March 7, 1919	Sampigny	Rest camp
November 11	Sampigny	Armistice

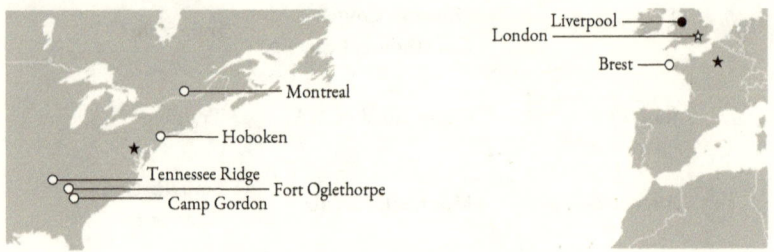

From the US and across the Atlantic.

Chronology

DATE	PLACE	EVENT
1919		
February 17	**Sampigny**	**Pershing inspects Thirty-Fifth Division**
March 10–April 4	Le Mans	Cantonment
April 12	**Brest**	**Embarkation *Manchuria***
April 23	**Hoboken, NJ, USA**	**Debarkation**
April 24	*Camp Upton, NY*	*Separated from Thirty-Fifth Division*
May 12	**Fort Oglethorpe, GA**	**Discharged**
May 14	Tennessee Ridge, TN	Homecoming

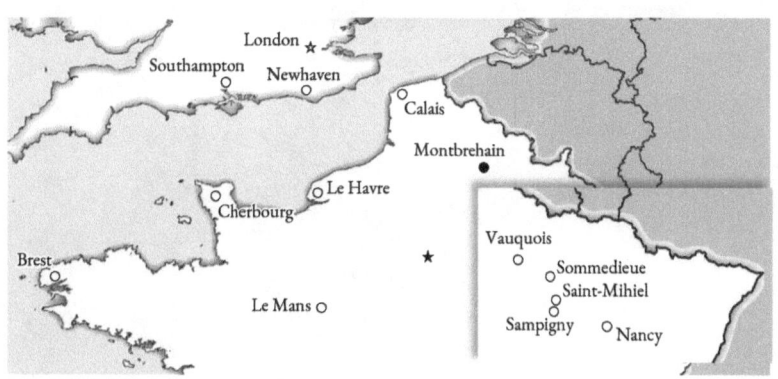

To the western front.

Part One

From Tennessee to the Great War

1   The Butte of Vauquois

Benjamin Franklin Potts was a US infantryman in the Meuse-Argonne Offensive, near Verdun, France, in 1918.

My Nanna once asked him, "Well, Daddy, what did you think about France?"

He said, "It's a very muddy place."

At twenty-four years old, B. F. Potts was a soldier in the 137th Infantry Regiment, which was part of the Thirty-Fifth Division. In September 1918, the Thirty-Fifth was ordered to take the "Vauquois Zone," a sector with a two-mile-wide front and, at its base, the Butte of Vauquois [pronounced *voh-kwa*].

The Butte of Vauquois is a hill rising 330 feet above the surrounding countryside. The hilltop provides a commanding view of the terrain on three sides, including the strategic railway from Verdun to Paris.

The Imperial German Army moved into Vauquois in early September 1914. The French took it back twelve days later. By the end of the month, the Germans tried to retake the hill, and the battle for the Butte of Vauquois began. The battle here would rage for four long years.

Before the war, a couple hundred people lived in the village of Vauquois at the top of the hill. From the start of the battle until the end, the hilltop was showered with artillery.

Butte of Vauquois, summit, August 2009. Trenches (*foreground*), mine craters (*middle*), and a monument to the combatants and the dead of Vauquois (*background*). Photo by the author.

After several months in place, German troops had constructed a network of trenches that, coupled with the steep terrain, made a formidable defense against ground attack. So, the French would dig a tunnel from a protected side of the hill to a position they gauged to be beneath enemy trenches, pack in a few tons of explosives, light the fuse, and run like hell. The resulting explosion would create a crater on the surface, its size corresponding to the amount of explosives used.

That's what "mining" means to a ground army. When the enemy catches on to what you're doing and starts listening to the ground and making their own tunnels beneath your tunnels and packing explosives into them—that's what they call "countermining."

The largest mine at Vauquois was set by the Germans. It contained sixty tons of explosives. It made a surface crater eighty feet deep and three hundred feet wide and killed 108 French soldiers in two lines of trenches. The war of mine-and-countermine went on for three years, until April of 1918.

By the time Private Potts arrived in September, France must have been a very muddy place, indeed.

After the war, the ground was littered with explosives and still is today. The former inhabitants of the hilltop village re-established their community at the foot of the hill.

2 Benjamin Potts Registers for the Draft

JUNE 5, 1917

In the spring of 1917, the Great War thundered across the fields of northern France. A large-scale Allied attack, called the Nivelle Offensive, failed with heavy casualties, resulting in a series of mutinies and mass desertions in the French Army. At the edge of the Argonne Forest, a battle of mine-and-countermine, now two years in, riddled the Butte of Vauquois with tunnels and craters.

On June 5, in the United States, ten million American men, ages twenty-one to thirty, signed their names to register to be drafted into military service. One of these was Benjamin Franklin Potts.

In the previous April, following the discovery that Germany was negotiating with Mexico to join the war against its northern neighbor, the United States declared war on the German Empire. The Selective Service Act of 1917 was enacted in May. It authorized the conscription of men to raise an army, allowing certain exclusions. Among them, having a dependent parent or a dependent sibling or child under twelve years of age was considered a good reason to be exempt from compulsory service.

In addition to this date, three other national registration days were held. One, on the same date a year later, to register men turned twenty-one during the year, followed by a second, August 24, for the same reason. The last, on the 12th of September, broadened the eligibility age, which became eighteen to forty-five.

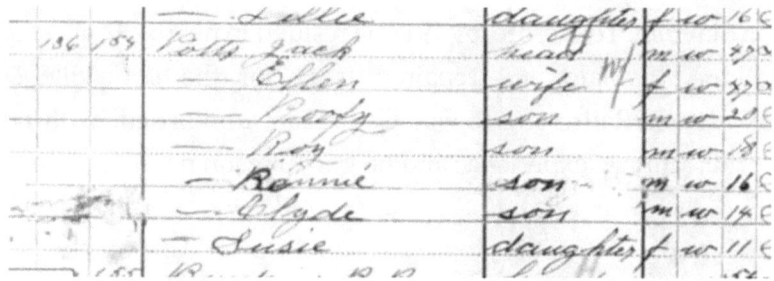

From the 1910 US census, which records nicknames "Bennie" and "Roofy," when Benjamin was sixteen years old, Rufus twenty.

All four sons of Jack and Ellen Potts were within the range. Benjamin Franklin, called "Bennie" by his family, was accompanied that day by his brothers, William "Roofy" Rufus, Roy Albert, and Clyde Brake.

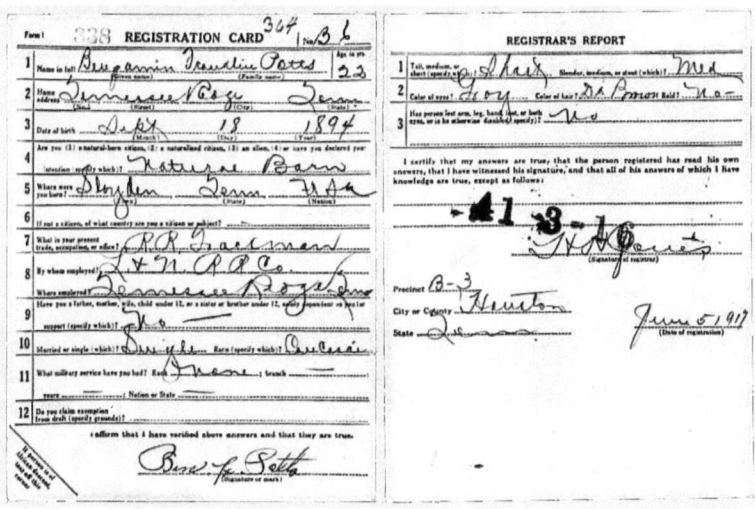

Draft registration card.

According to his draft registration card, B. F. Potts was twenty-two years old, short in height, medium in build. He had gray eyes and dark brown hair. Born September 18, 1894, in Slayden, Tennessee, by 1917 he resided in nearby Tennessee Ridge. He laid and repaired track for the Louisville & Nashville Railroad. He was Caucasian, unmarried, with no prior military experience and no good reason not to get some.

3   Military Induction and Entrainment

June 27, 1918

"I, Benjamin Franklin Potts, do solemnly swear that I will support the constitution of the United States."

The words feel like strangers in the mouth, being, at the same time, repeated after a man in uniform and of such moral import.

The American flag on his right, the Tennessee Tristar, left, an army officer stands before a group of young men. They are farmers, teachers, laborers, and railroad men. All dressed in their best clothes, they're aligned in loose ranks. A small suitcase or a simple bag, containing a change of clothes and a shaving kit, sits on the floor to each man's left. Their right hands are raised, palms out.

The officer continues: "I—State your name...."

"I, Benjamin Franklin Potts, do solemnly swear to bear true allegiance to the United States of America, and to serve them honestly and faithfully, against all their enemies or opposers whatsoever, and to observe and obey the orders of the President of the United States of America, and the orders of the officers appointed over me."

June 27, 1918, B. F. Potts spoke these words, right hand raised, at the Houston County Court House in Erin, Tennessee, and so became a private in the US Army.

The two oaths, taken by all commissioned and noncommissioned officers and privates, were defined by the

First United States Congress in 1789. The oath for officers changed over the years, but the oaths for enlisted men stayed the same until the mid-twentieth century.

Following the brief ceremony, Private Potts was escorted onto a train with several dozen other draftees. On boarding, each man was given two box lunches, supplied by the Red Cross Society of Erin, that would be his dinner and supper. The train pulled out for Camp Gordon in Chamblee, Georgia, where the men would undergo six weeks of military training.

Three months from that day, B. F. Potts would be fighting in France.

Two of Ben's three brothers were also drafted for the war. Nine months prior, Roy Albert, two years Ben's senior, took the same train to Camp Gordon. The youngest, Clyde Brake, would leave for Camp Wadsworth near Spartanburg, South Carolina, in September. Only the eldest, William Rufus, was excluded from the draft, being married with three young children at the time.

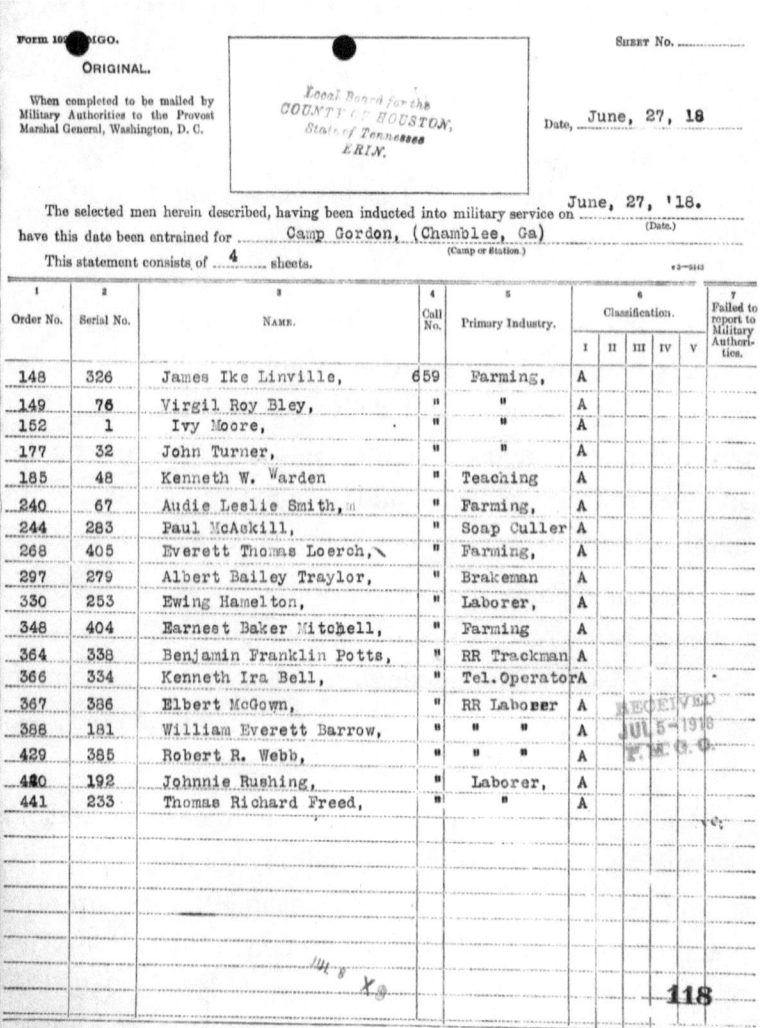

Induction and entrainment, Form 1029, Provost Marshal General Office, showing Benjamin Franklin Potts, Order No. 364, was inducted into military service and entrained for Camp Gordon June 27, 1918. The reverse (*not shown*) indicates his arrival June 29.

4   Army Training at Camp Gordon

July-August 1918

"If it moves, salute it. If it doesn't move, paint it!"

For the officers and noncommissioned officers in charge, military training is an exercise in organization. Equipment must be requisitioned and delivered to the training field; trainees must be housed, clothed, and fed three times a day, and they must be moved to and from the training site. Actual training takes place only a few hours each day.

For the soldier, then, military training is an exercise in patience. But while a soldier waits, the devil called boredom is his companion, and morale suffers. Busy work is a common solution. The quote above stuck with Ben's twin boys, Jesse and Wesley, because their father often recited it.

Camp Gordon in Chamblee, northeast of Atlanta, Georgia, was one of thirty-two military training camps that sprang up near America's large cities in 1917. As part of his War Preparedness Movement developed in 1914 while he was Army Chief of Staff, General Leonard Wood called for training camps to be built near cities with rail access and a large water supply.

Soon after the declaration of war, the camps were under construction as trainees were moving in. All those clapboard buildings needed painting. As did the stones that marked the borders of roads and walkways.

During the first days of training in that hot, humid Georgia July of 1918, Private Potts and his comrades learned military courtesy and drill and ceremony, instilling the high degree of discipline required of a soldier. Later, they learned the use of arms. Most American boys of the era were familiar with hunting rifles, which is fortunate since, due to lack of equipment, they often trained with wooden stakes.

Barracks at Camp Gordon (postcard, c. 1917).

The latter part of the six-week training period included two divergent forms of combat tactics—maneuver and trench warfare. In the early days of the Great War, the Allies employed maneuver warfare to combat the invading German army, pushing it back or recoiling before its advance. But improved technology, notably more accurate, mobile artillery and the machine gun, made the battlefield a more lethal environment than in previous wars. The Allies dug in to secure their gains or prevent further losses.

Trench warfare led to what General John J. Pershing, Commander of the American Expeditionary Force (AEF), called "abnormal stabilized warfare." Pershing believed the stalemate in Europe was the logical outcome of the defensive tactics that define trench warfare.

Pershing advocated, not formations facing-off in open fields as in battles of the American Civil War, but large-unit maneuver tactics, where the infantry advances through opposing lines, pushing the enemy off the field. At the same time, the general acknowledged the role of trench warfare and allowed for its basic instruction in the training program.

Abandoned in 1921, the Camp Gordon site became a naval air station during World War II. Today, a plaque among the hangars of Dekalb Peachtree Airport marks the site of the World War I training camp.

5 Embarkation, the *Tunisian*, and the Bridge of Ships

AUGUST 24, 1918

Potts, Benjamin F., PVT. INF., Army Serial Number 3501865, and other members of Camp Gordon August Automatic Replacement Draft Company #11, Infantry, boarded the *Tunisian* at Montreal on August 24, 1918, bound for the war in Europe.

It was in the summer of 1918 when General Pershing promised the men that, by Christmas, they'd be in "Heaven, Hell, or Hoboken."

As the Headquarters Port of Embarkation, Hoboken, New Jersey, was where many American troops shipped off to war, and as the port where they hoped afterward to return, it became a homecoming emblem. It was already a busy port before 1917, but when the army began to move men and equipment through it as well, the supporting rail system bogged down in gridlock. To relieve congestion, subports were opened in the US at Boston, Baltimore, and Philadelphia and in Canada at Halifax, St. Johns, and Montreal.

To transport the two million soldiers that eventually made up the AEF in Europe along with the necessary equipment in a timely manner, war planners knew, would require a veritable "bridge of ships." To that end, the US government ordered the construction of new ships, commandeered American cruise liners, borrowed ships from Great Britain and Canada, and seized enemy vessels.

The steamship *Tunisian* was built by Alexander Stephen & Sons for the Allan Line Steamship Company of Glasgow and launched at Princess Dock on the River Clyde, near Greenock, Scotland, January 17, 1900.

The *Tunisian* on trials, the River Clyde, 1900.

Five hundred feet long with a fifty-nine-foot beam (a ship's widest point at the waterline), it could accommodate 1,460 civilian passengers on four decks. At a cruising speed of sixteen knots, like most commercial steamers of the time, it could keep pace with contemporary warships (Smith, *Trans-Atlantic Passenger Ships*, 177).

In magazine advertisements during its commercial career, the *Tunisian* is described as a "luxurious cabin steamer." During the war, it served as a prisoner-of-war ship and a troop transport for Canadian and American forces.

HEADQUARTERS PORT OF EMBARKATION, HOBOKEN, NEW JERSEY
PASSENGER LIST OF ORGANIZATIONS AND CASUALS

Sheet No. 10
3RD Class

CAMP GORDON AUGUST AUTOMATIC REPLACEMENT
DRAFT, COMPANY # 41, INFANTRY
I-575-S
MONTREAL
TUNISIAN
AUG 24 1918

No.	NAME	Corps. Ex'pl'n. Capt. QMRC	Organization	NOTIFY IN CASE OF EMERGENCY	Relationship	ADDRESS
163.	PATTON, JAMES. 2557704	PVT. INF.		MRS. ROSE PATTON	MOTH.	6912 WAKEFIELD AVE. CLEVELAND, OHIO.
164.	PAYNE, THOMAS D. 3501791	"		F. FRANCIS M. PAYNE	FATH.	R.F.D.# 2, LUCY, TENN.
165.	PERSIN, CHRIST. 3502544	"		MRS. MINNIE G. PERSIN	MOTH.	4410 LESTER AVE., CLEVELAND, OHIO.
166.	PFAHL, JOHN A. 3502511.	"		MRS. ANNA B. PFAHL	MOTH.	1925 WALTON AVE., CLEVELAND, O.
167.	PHILLIPS, CHARLES D. 3497754	"		MISS MARY W. PHILLIPS	SIS.	123 E. RICHARDSON ST ATLANTA, GA.
168.	PHIPPS, CHARLEY E. 3500757	"		GEORGE D. PHIPPS	FATH.	SPRINGFIELD, TENN.
169.	PICKENS, WILLIAM T. 3497756	"		WILLIAM PICKENS	FATH.	LILBURN, GA.
170.	PICKETT, ORVILLE J. 3502464	"		MRS. MARGARET P. PICKETT	MOTH.	1157 E. 72ND ST., CLEVELAND, O.
171.	PIERSON, WAIDE H. 3500977	"		JAMES L. PIERSON	FATH.	R.F.D.# 1. MELROSE, TENN.
172.	PINKSTON, GARRETT G. 3500816	"		TURNER PINKSTON	FATH.	BRYANT STATION, TENN.
173.	POCUKONIS, JULIUS 3466308	"		WILLIAM CITRAICUS (HALF-BRO)		2139 W. 61ST ST., CLEVELAND, OHIO.
174.	POOLE, ELBERT. 3500702	"		MRS. LIZZIE B. POOLE	WIFE.	R.F.D.# THOMASVILLE, TENN.
175.	POTTS, BENJAMIN F. 3501866	"		ALBERT POTTS	FATH.	TENNESSEE RIDGE, TENN.
176.	PREWETT, HUGH P. 3501797	"		MRS. MAMIE PREWETT	WIFE.	R.F.D.# 5, CARTERSVILLE, GA.
177.	PRICE, WALTER N. 3497860	"		OLIVER S. PRICE	FATH.	62 N. PRYOR ST., ATLANTA, GA.
178.	PURCELL, JAMES M. 3501933	"		THOMAS P. PURCELL	FATH.	R.F.D.# 1. AUSTELL, GA.
179.	RASSMAN, WILLIAM E. 3500776	"		MRS. ELSIE F. RASSMAN	WIFE.	BUMPUS MILLS, TENN.
180.	REED, LESLIE C. 2252855	"		WILLIAM C. REED	FATH.	GRAHAM, TEXAS.

DISPOSITION:
Five copies of this list to be handed to the representative of embarkation personnel adjutant's office at gangplank by which company embarks.

(Signature of Company Commander.)
(Rank.)

From the *Tunisian*'s passenger list, August 24, 1918.

Leaving London, August 7, 1918, it docked in Montreal August 19, disembarking 241 civilians, listed as tourists. Five days later, it steamed down the Saint Lawrence carrying US troops.

The passenger list doesn't show the destination port or the arrival date. But another soldier, Sergeant Raymond Gerbracht of Livingston County, Illinois, was also aboard. After the war, the Livingston County Board of Supervisors published a book containing the service records of local servicemen. *Livingston County Illinois in the World War* gives Gerbracht's itinerary: "Sailed from Montreal, Canada, August 24, 1918, on *Tunisian*. Landed at London, England, September 8, 1918" (Sparks, 202).

In his first ocean voyage, B. F. Potts crossed the submarine-infested waters of the North Atlantic in a convoy of steamers escorted by a warship. He passed the long summer days scrubbing the decks, responding to boat drills and fire drills, and trying not to be sick. At night, no lights and no smoking were allowed on deck. The crossing from Montreal to London took fifteen days, during which time a life vest, made of cork, was his constant companion.

After the war, the *Tunisian* continued its passenger route as part of the Canadian Pacific Line. It was converted from steam to oil fuel in 1921 and in 1922 renamed the *Marburn*. As the *Marburn*, the ship finished its career, scrapped at Genoa, in 1928.

6 Enterprise, Tennessee

My great uncle John Wesley Potts, one of Ben Potts's twins, was the family genealogist. To him the Potts family is thankful for much of the information we have concerning the family history. I have several photocopied pages of the family tree, which include old photographs and a few stories. These last are in Uncle Wesley's words, typed by his hand.

I'm fond of one story in particular. It reminds me of a favorite Dr. Seuss book, and like *The Lorax*, it remains pertinent. As it gives context to the childhood of our present subject, it is appropriate at this point to transcribe the story of a town named Enterprise as told by John Wesley Potts.

Enterprise, Tennessee: The Town That Died

Enterprise was a sawmill town on the banks of Lewis Branch. Around 1900, there were sawmills, [making] stave and shingles. The town was aptly named because it was growing. It grew in size from 200 to 300 people.

The timber was plentiful. Virgin oak, ash, beach and hickory.

Grandpa Albert Jack Potts moved his family there in 1901 from Slayden, Tennessee.

Grandpa was a teamster. He owned matched pairs of horses. Him and the boys [Ben and his brothers] cut and snaked logs out of the woods to the roads. He got a dollar a day plus fifty cents for the horses.

In a few short years the timber was cut, and the town slowly fell apart, much like the lumber towns of Upper Michigan. Grandpa stayed in Houston County and bought a farm. He lived there until his death, at 64, in 1929. Albert Jack and Lou Ellen Potts are buried in the McDonald Cemetery along with four of their children.

Pa would marvel at the way they lumber today.

John Wesley Potts
1927-2015

7 Rendezvous with the Thirty-Fifth Division

September 11, 1918

Grandpa Ben told me about a time on a train in France. They had stopped for the night and were directed to stay on the train, which was on a track next to a small French town. Some of the guys disobeyed orders, went into the town, broke into a bakery, and stole all the bread and baked goods. When the baker discovered the theft in the morning, he complained to the officer in charge. Restitution was paid to the baker, and Grandpa said the [soldiers'] punishment was severe.

—*Bruce Potts*

I've found no official records concerning Benjamin Franklin Potts during his time in France. A fire in 1973 at the National Personnel Records Center in St. Louis, Missouri, destroyed the service records of eighteen million US Army and Air Force personnel discharged from 1912 to 1964.

The next chronological document I have is his return voyage from France in April 1919. So, if we are to continue the journey, we must turn to other sources.

His discharge paper shows B. F. Potts was a member of Company M, 137th Infantry. The 137th Regiment was part of the Thirty-Fifth Infantry Division, which fought in *Les Vosges* [pronounced with a soft *g*: *lay vohzh*], the Meuse [sounds like "mud" with a *z*: *muz*], and the Argonne Forest.

The Thirty-Fifth Infantry Division was composed of Kansas and Missouri National Guard units. The division was organized into two infantry brigades, plus support units, including the Sixtieth Field Artillery Brigade and the 110th Engineer Regiment.

American troops headed for the trenches, 1918 (King et al., *Spearhead of Logistics*, 108). French rail cars were called "Forty-and-Eights" after their carrying capacity, stenciled on the side: "HOMMES 40 : CHEVAUX (en long) 8"—forty men, eight (longwise) horses.

The two infantry brigades contained two regiments each. The Sixty-Ninth Brigade consisted of the 137th and 138th Regiments. The Seventieth Brigade, the 139th and 140th. Each regiment was further divided into twelve 250-man companies, identified by letters *A* through *M*. (Traditionally, there was no Company J, because, in older type, the letter resembled an *I*.) The 137th Infantry Regiment, constituted entirely of proud Kansas National Guardsmen, was nicknamed the "All Kansas."

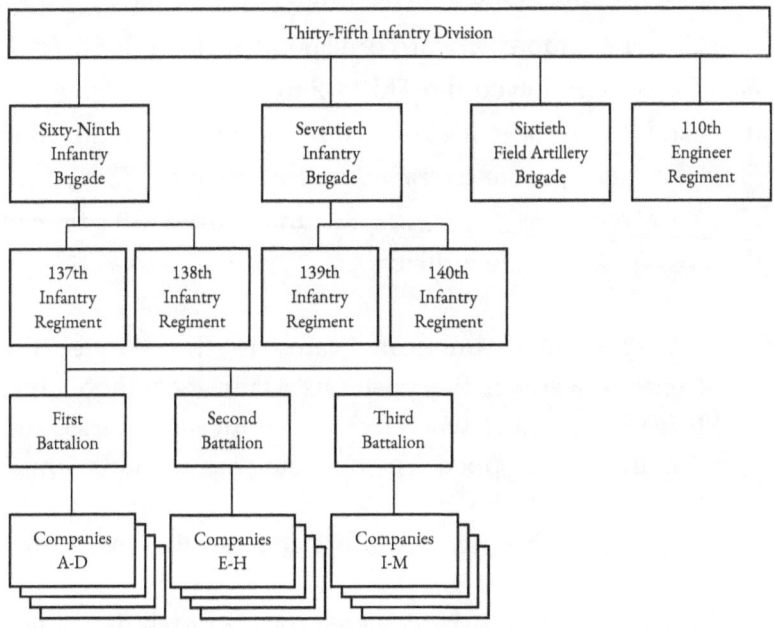

Thirty-Fifth Division order of battle (partial). This chart shows only the units pertinent to our story. The battalion and company levels are typical of infantry regiments.

Federalized on August 5, 1917, the Thirty-Fifth Division began training in September that year at Camp Doniphan, Fort Sill, Oklahoma. It left Hoboken, New Jersey, for Europe April 25, 1918. From Liverpool, across the English countryside to Southampton, it crossed the Channel and arrived at Le Havre, France, sixteen days later, on May 11.

The division's first posting in the trenches was in the Vosges, south of Verdun. This was a "quiet sector," that is, the line had to be held, but advancement by either side was of little strategic importance. Raw troops were sent there for practical training in the trench warfare environment.

Clair Kenamore, a war correspondent for the *St. Louis Post-Dispatch*, followed the Thirty-Fifth Division throughout the war. He tells the stories of its officers and men in the book *From Vauquois Hill to Exermont: A History of the Thirty-Fifth Division of the United States Army*. Of the Thirty-Fifth's time in the Vosges, Kenamore writes:

> When the Americans came to the Vosges, the trenches were in the positions established more than three years before when the French invaded Alsace and dug in when stopped. The opposing armies had seemed to agree that the decision would be gained to the northwest, on other fields of fame, so they sent tired troops to the Vosges to rest or filled the line with territorials. A few shells were sent over each day, a few infrequent raids were made at night to learn what troops were opposite, wire was kept in good shape and trenches and dugouts were maintained in good repair, but little beyond this was done. The great war was allowed to rage elsewhere. No men were sacrificed in this part of the world. (52)

After disembarking the *Tunisian* at London on the 8th of September, B. F. Potts entrained to England's south coast, at Southampton or Newhaven, then crossed the English Channel to a French port, most likely at Le Havre, Cherbourg, or Calais. From the coast, another train, this one of Forty-and-

Eights, took him to meet his unit in the country's northeast. The entire trip from London to the rendezvous with the Thirty-Fifth could have taken as little as three days, arriving September 11.

The dates and places in the previous paragraph are conjecture, derived from similar (documented) journeys of AEF units. The intent is to arrive at the earliest date Private Potts could have joined the division.

The Thirty-Fifth Division left the Vosges by September 3 and moved into the area of Rosières-aux-Salines [*rozy-air oh sal-een*]. There, they rested until September 10. According to Kenamore:

> The march of the night of Sept. 10-11 was into Tomblaine, Jarville and Maron, which are suburbs of Nancy.... The next night [of the 11th] the division marched again—through the edge of the city of Nancy and into the Forest de Haye, where they went into concealed bivouac. (71)

Since there weren't many—if any—train rides once he gained the front, the story Grandpa Ben told Bruce at this chapter's opening probably occurred during the transfer from the coast to the rendezvous point.

> But we left about 100 of our men there in the foothills of the Alps [the Vosges]. They were killed in action, died of wounds or of disease or accident. I had not realized the number was so large until I came to count them up. It shows how heavy is the toll of war even in the quietest of sectors. (65)

B. F. Potts replaced one of those hundred men.

Up to that time, only Company C of the 137th had experienced combat, having executed a successful raid on German trenches in July. When he joined them in early September, Private Potts's comrades in Company M, though hardened to field rations, going without a bath, and marching in mud, were as green as he was. We might imagine the Kansas boys gave the Tennessean a hard time anyway.

8 In Reserve at Saint-Mihiel

SEPTEMBER 12, 1918

That first of September was a notable day, although it did not appear so at the time, for it was the last time the men were to sleep under cover for more than a month, and that month the most trying in their histories. (Kenamore, 69)

By the time Private B. F. Potts joined the Thirty-Fifth Infantry Division, they had spent their last night indoors. According to Kenamore's account and others, rain fell on the region during much of September. In the hurried preparations for battle, sit-down meals, showers, and even a change of clothes were not to be had for the coming weeks.

Resting during the day, the Thirty-Fifth Division troops marched through the nights of September 10 and 11. In *Heroes of the Argonne: An Authentic History of the Thirty-Fifth Division*, author Charles B. Hoyt describes the scene:

> There are no lights, for smoking is forbidden where there is danger of enemy planes swooping down at any minute. There are no noises, save for the jangling of accoutrement and the crunch of the hobnailed soldier. On such marches the soldiers do not talk much among themselves. They have rifles and seventy-pound packs to think about. What more could be asked to keep one's mind occupied?
>
> The road is jammed with moving troops. The advance is made by paces. The men take the distance of a

few yardsticks ahead; then stop, and stand in inactivity while a cold drizzle washes their faces and adds pounds to their packs.

The men wear out as the night wears on. Their clothing is saturated; their packs weigh over the seventy pounds now; and shoulders are numbed. When the column halts, they halt in their tracks and slump into the mud. (54)

Marching into reserve at Saint-Mihiel (Hoyt, 55).

On the morning of September 12, the division moved into the Forest of Haye, west of Nancy.

Not three months before, Bennie Potts was a railroad man in the quiet hills of Tennessee. Now, Private Potts is an infantryman in France, a land ripped open by four years of war.

It is an extraordinary sensation to find oneself in a strange place, a foreign country, as well as in a military environment, where every action is an order, direct or implied. What's more, it's a hazardous place, where accidents maim and kill, where disease lurks, where the rain is often made in metal and brings explosive flowers that smell of poison gas.

Memories of home and family, childhood images, bright fields, shaded woods, his father cutting timber on a riverbank, himself leading a workhorse, trailing logs between trees—all fade against the stark landscape. Slight hills fold into one another, long, low lines devoid of silhouettes. The trees here have lost leaves as well as branches, as if in a hellish storm.

Remembering his training, remembering the movements, the sequence of actions, forgetting the green Georgia woods where they were pressed into the mind, the soldier follows orders. He concentrates on the job at hand, does what must be done, right now. Of the past and of the future, he thinks not—he dares not, lest a moment's distraction at a critical instant deprive him of all past memories and of any future whatsoever.

While the Americans fought smaller engagements and played a significant role in the Aisne-Marne campaign in July and August, up to now the divisions, led by American generals, had fallen under the command of French and British corps commanders. One of General Pershing's objectives as AEF commander was to establish an independent American army, which he did on August 10, 1918.

By September, Pershing pointed the American First Army, over one million strong, at the Saint-Mihiel salient. A "salient," in military terms, is a bulge in the front line. Because a salient's defenders are exposed on three sides, the situation is tolerated only if the area contains strategic terrain.

Resulting from a German offensive in September 1914, the St. Mihiel salient was a 200-square-mile triangle jutting fourteen miles into the Allied lines between the Moselle and Meuse rivers. Bounded by Pont-à-Mousson to the south, St. Mihiel to the west, and the Verdun area to the north, the terrain was mostly rolling plain, heavily wooded in spots. After three years of occupation, the Germans had turned the area into a fortress with heavy bands of barbed wire and strong artillery and machine-gun emplacements. Eight divisions defended the salient, with five more in reserve. (Stuart, *American Military History*, 42)

The battle of Saint-Mihiel, which took place September 12-15, was Pershing's first operation as army commander. He assigned the Thirty-Fifth to the strategic reserve, whose purpose is to replace a weakened unit, to fill any gap in the line created by the enemy, or to take advantage of such a gap created by friendly forces. The Germans learned details of the impending attack, including the size of the opposing force, which was much superior to their own. As the Americans launched the offensive, the German army was in retreat. The battle, against the disorganized enemy, was executed according to plan. Pershing didn't need the reserve. The division waited under rain.

The troops of the Thirty-Fifth would be "blooded" soon enough; the future was saving them for a greater fight. Eleven days after the battle of Saint-Mihiel, they would be in the line before the Butte of Vauquois, one of the most heavily defended points in the German line. The Meuse-Argonne Offensive would be the decisive battle of the Great War.

9 A Soldier's Sentiment

September 12-15, 1918

Prior to battle, musical instruments are confiscated and stored, and army band members become guards, messengers, first aid providers, and stretcher-bearers.

Kenamore attests to their valor:

> The wounded were carried by members of the band, whose work throughout brought praise from all officers, and men who saw it. These men without arms and without identifying brassards, took their stretchers onto the field, watched the work of their fighting comrades, and bore the wounded back up the steep slope. The position of an unarmed man on a battlefield is always a most trying one, but these musicians worked magnificently. (62)

Carl E. Haterius was a horn player in the 137th Regiment band. Though forbidden in order to protect operational security, he kept a journal throughout his military service. After the war, he compiled the entries into a book, *Reminiscences of the 137th U. S. Infantry*. In it, he records the ambiance of the wartime environment and provides insight into the soldier's life.

While the Thirty-Fifth Division waited in reserve in the Haye Forest, Haterius made notes that became the following passage. Though it is perhaps long-winded for our time, I cite its entirety. For it expresses a sentiment with which, I suspect, a soldier who has "passed through the inferno" can identify, and from which family members might gain understanding.

Our life here in this forest was a dismal one, and in passing I might add, that often as we lay there in our little pup tents during some dark night listening to the patter of raindrops on our little canvas tents, our thoughts would often revert back over the miles of cruel distance, far back across the ocean, and out to where the "West begins." We were now learning the grimness of war and were commencing to realize that it was no child's play. It called for men, big, strong, robust, vigorous, strong-hearted men. It was no place for a weakling. The "mind willing but the flesh weak" did not harmonize in our picture. Many times, when conditions were almost unbearable, we must needs urge ourselves onward, with little time for the thought of home or old environs, for to have given an absolute free rein to our thoughts and emotions would have proved a difficult handicap to overcome. The less we thought about it the better off we were. It was no use in becoming more miserable than we were at times. Many times, while sitting in some lowly billet or bivouacked in some dark, overshadowing wood, and while writing to loved ones at home, we would intentionally leave out much concerning our life at that particular time. Many stories sent back home were but half told. They must not know, as it would only cause their anxiety to increase. Those at home were fighting their battle, and sometimes I have been inclined to believe that theirs was the hardest battle. No one will ever know just what the fathers, mothers, wives and other loved ones suffered. They in turn bore their burdens in silence, and little was said or made known. The spirit of all was wonderful to behold. Even over there time after time that home feeling would creep into our souls like a thief in the night. We were but human after all. Those times were perhaps the hardest battles we had to fight. Only a soldier who has been over there and passed through the inferno can realize the meaning of these lines. (118-119)

10 Special Job for Private Potts

It's difficult to imagine the Grandpa I knew as a young man, in the prime of youth, in the uniform of a World War I infantryman. But there he is.

Private Potts's medium frame fills the olive drab wool service tunic, with narrow, standing collar, five buttons up the front, and dressed over matching breeches. Russet colored leather leggings wrap the calves, topping hobnailed brogan boots, also russet leather. The private's rank is shown by the lack of insignia on his sleeve.

Unseen, a pair of aluminum tags hangs around his neck on a cord, tucked beneath the tunic. Each, the size of a half dollar, is stamped with the soldier's name, rank, serial number, and unit. In the event of his death, one of these tags stays with the body, while the other is used to record the casualty. This grim necklace would be removed for the last time by Ben Potts, civilian.

The wide brim of a shallow-crowned steel helmet, fastened with a leather chin strap, shields blue eyes from the sun or, more often, from rain. When the soldier finds occasion to grin, his ears perk up, raising the brim.

Like the WWII and Vietnam-era "steel pot" helmet with which we're familiar from so many movies, the WWI helmet, with its characteristic wide brim, wasn't intended to stop bullets. It would protect the head from flying debris, including shrapnel—sometimes. Not until the introduction of the Kevlar helmet in 1983 could a soldier hope his headgear might keep high-velocity lead outside the brain pan.

It's in company formation where Private B. F. Potts stands out. In the ranks, every man looks identical: standing at attention, heels together, arms to the sides, fingers curled, chin up, chest out, shoulders back, stomach in, eyes front. Inspecting the troops prior to battle, a captain peers down at the top of a helmet.

"Private Potts, how tall are you?"

The soldier, looking into a button of the captain's coat, says, "Five foot three, sir." The wide brim raises.

In the maneuver warfare that would push the opponent from the field and, thereby, win the war, soldiers often meet the enemy in hand-to-hand combat. The rifle, bayonet fixed, becomes a spear and a club. This is a contest between "the quick and the dead." It is a contest won by larger men.

Also in maneuver warfare, communication between commanders on the battlefield is key to victory. Orders are given and units move forward, engaging the enemy. As the battle develops, orders are changed; new orders must be given. Whereas wires link telephones in the trenches, no such luxury is afforded commanders of units on the move. These commanders write orders and messages on paper and rely on an agile—and often lucky—soldier to avoid artillery, bullets, and getting lost to deliver the missive.

The messenger is often called a "runner." The soldier with a low profile makes a better runner.

"Fall out, Private Potts. I have a special job for you."

Hand-to-hand combat training (postcard, c. 1917).

In one of Grandpa's oft cited stories (which will be told in due course), the infantryman, wishing to visit his brother in a field hospital, gets permission from a certain artillery officer. In another story, the private is alone when he encounters an enemy soldier.

If we are to accept the man's hundred-year-old stories as truth—and if we do not, we might as well have not set out on our present journey—then we may desire to render plausible the infantryman's connection to the artillery officer, as well as the solo encounter with the enemy. I propose that Private Potts was selected to be a runner.

At my prompting, Bruce asked Uncle Jesse if this could be the case. The response was affirmative. Bruce writes:

> *He was a messenger, traveling from camp to camp, often under fire when he was crawling through fields.*

Here, we are accepting the risk that, instead of prompting the recollection with the question, we created a false memory. That Private Potts was a runner is, as far as I'm aware, new information, albeit obtained secondhand and a hundred years after the fact. Skepticism on that point is justified. The anecdotes remain.

11 Another Wednesday in the War

September 18, 1918

The 18th of September was a Wednesday. It was the day Benjamin Franklin Potts turned twenty-four years old. Any letters from home wishing him a happy birthday would have found him around Foucaucourt-sur-Thabas, six miles west of Les Charmentois, sixteen miles south of the Butte of Vauquois.

Happy Birthday, Bennie.

12 A Potts Family Day of Thanks

SEPTEMBER 19, 1918

> *One day they came upon a building during a rainstorm, and the guys wanted to seek shelter there. The captain forbade them from entering, so they slept in the field that night about a hundred yards away. In the middle of the night, the building was destroyed by an artillery shell, and Ben received a dent in his helmet from what he thought was a piece of wood.*
>
> —*Bruce Potts*

September 15, 1918, the Thirty-Fifth Infantry Division moved during the night, as all movement now must be kept secret from enemy surveillance, into the Charmentois [*sharm-on-twa*] area on "motorbuses." Kenamore describes the vehicles as follows:

> those immense lumbering cars which were stripped from the streets of London and Paris at the beginning of the war, and which had rambled all over the North of France since, hauling soldiers to many threatened fields, carrying wounded back and at times playing the part of trucks and taking supplies forward. (72)

Maybe Benjamin Potts and his buddies made jokes and pretended to be tourists, tipping their helmets back, pointing out the windows, imagining a more lovely landscape beyond the darkness.

"My goodness, Henrietta, have you ever seen such beautiful scenery?" says one soldier.

Another replies in falsetto, "Never in my life, George. I'm so glad you convinced me to go on vacation in France!"

"Most folks prefer the south of France," says another, "but I must say the north is more to my liking."

And still another, "All this sightseeing makes a man thirsty—*Garse-on, ewn bee-air, see voo play!*"

Maybe they all had a good laugh. Maybe they slept.

At this stopping place [Charmentois], which also was out of doors, the air bombs became more frequent.

The Sixty-ninth Brigade [including Private Potts's 137th Regiment] moved up near Auzeville [*oh-zay-veel*] on the night of Sept. 19-20, and the next night the remainder of the division went to the neighborhood of Grange-le-Comte Farm and into the woods east of Beauchamp, where the division relieved the Seventy-third French Division in charge of the sector. (72)

This movement was on foot. On the front now, the Thirty-Fifth was in range of artillery fire, and enemy planes made nighttime bombing raids over the countryside. The night of September 19 may be the earliest occasion for an officer's order, a soldier's discipline, and Private Potts's steel helmet to take the dent in place of his skull.

I wonder, if it had happened differently, in what body would my soul now inhabit?

Partial map sheet (*opposite*): *Bar-le-Duc, Partie N. E. La carte de l'état-major* (Dépôt de la Guerre, 1866).

The map shows the area around Auzéville, France, including Grange-le-Comte Farm (*right*) and Beauchamp (*lower left*). Compared to a current satellite image, the area appears little changed.

The 273 rectangular sheets that constitute *La carte de l'état-major* cover all of France at 1:40,000 scale. Elevation (in meters) is marked on hilltops and mountain peaks. Steepness is indicated by hatch marks, lines like rays from a peak. The closer together these lines, the steeper the slope. This elevation hatching and the Garamond typeface make the maps distinctive.

In use from the mid-nineteenth to well into the twentieth century, these maps were used by the French Army during the war to generate larger scale maps of the western front.

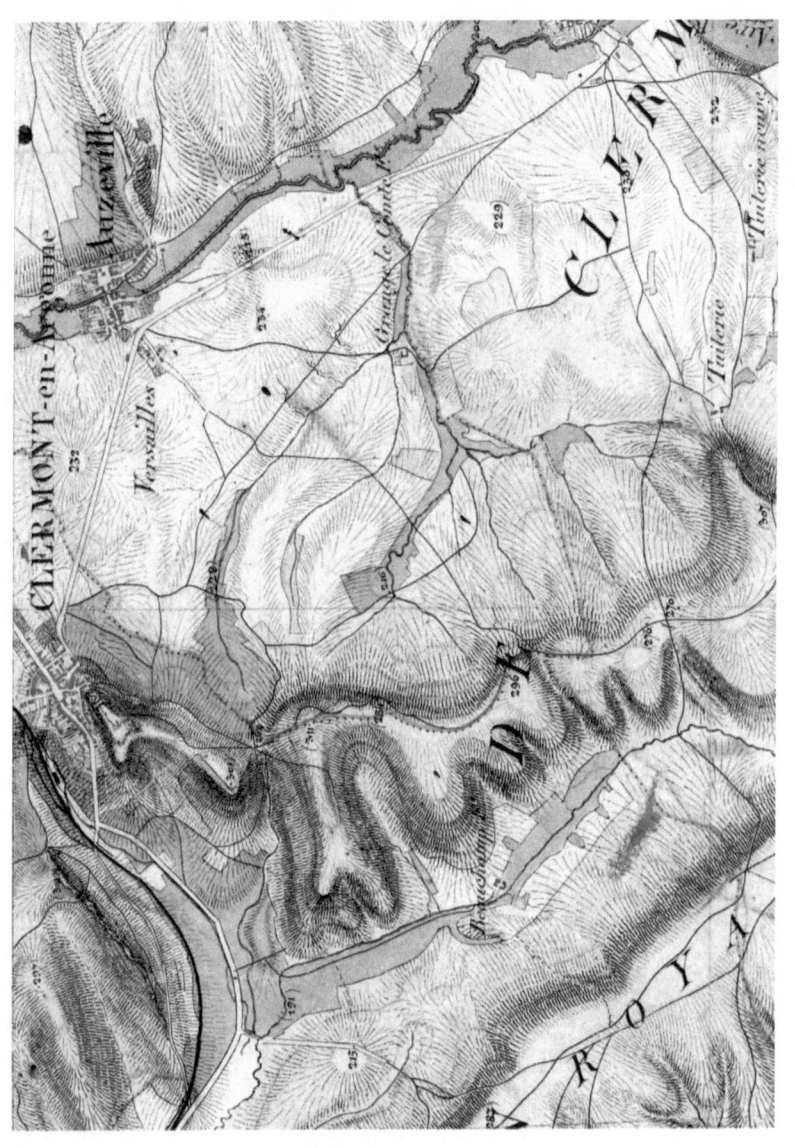

PART TWO

THE ARGONNE BATTLE

Map (*opposite*): *Grange-le-Comte Sector, September 21-25, 1918; Meuse-Argonne Offensive, September 26-October 3, 1918* (American Battle Monuments Commission, 1937).

Here, we can see where B. F. Potts would have been on any given day, September 26-30, 1918.

The map shows the area through which the Thirty-Fifth Division advanced in the first days of the Meuse-Argonne Offensive. The two thick, vertical lines mark the boundaries of the division sector, left and right. The ragged horizontal lines show the limit of advance at midnight on the date indicated.

A one-kilometer (0.62 miles) grid delineates the terrain. Contour lines show elevation in five-meter (16.4 feet) intervals.

To this map and to enlarged sections which follow, I've added labels for clarity. See also bibliography.

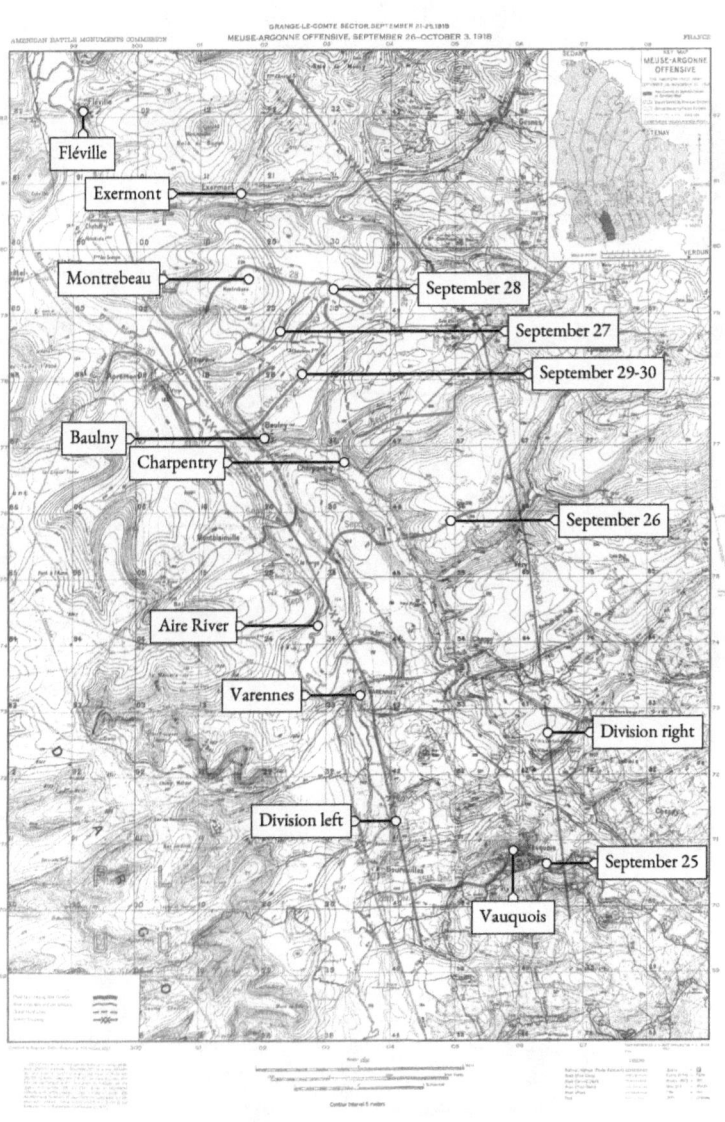

13 Planning the Meuse-Argonne Offensive

September 24, 1918

Detailed below is the battle plan where it concerns Private B. F. Potts of Company M, 137th Infantry Regiment. For the moment, we rely on Kenamore, who ably describes the stakes in the Meuse-Argonne Offensive, which begins two days hence.

At the conference of allied leaders when the great general attack was planned, the French commander in chief asked:

"Where will the American army fight in this battle?"

"Wherever you wish it to fight," Gen. Pershing replied.

Gen. Foch then indicated the line between the Meuse and the Argonne and asked if they would take that part of the line. Gen. Pershing assented. It was the part of the line where the heaviest fighting undoubtedly would be if the battle plans worked out, and if the judgment of the military men proved true. Every officer present knew that. The allies were at a point in the operation where a continuation of their strokes would drive the enemy out of France, or he would suffer disaster, possibly annihilation of his armies in the field. To get his armies out, he must maintain his [line of] communications, the four-track railroad at Mezieres in front of us, and the business of the Americans was to threaten, and if possible, to cut [this line].

It was a field where there was a certainty of the hardest fighting. It was probable that the Germans would bring their best battalions there to make the vital fight. As a consequence, there could be no spectacular gains on the American front. Every foot of ground would be contested bitterly, and those who advanced must pay the price. While on other fronts, large and glittering gains would be made in a day, it would be against a retreating foe, and he would be retreating all the more hurriedly because of the pressure the Americans were bringing on his vitals. The enemy could not retreat on our front. If he did, we would cut his railroads and the French and British to the west of us would capture his armies. It was with a full understanding of what was ahead that the American commander took this post of high honor, where hard blows were to be given and taken, and where there was little to gain. (76-77)

Between the rivers Aisne and Meuse, the First, Third, and Fifth Corps of the American First Army were positioned across a twenty-mile front. Each corps had three divisions on the line. First Corps' Seventy-Seventh, Twenty-Eighth, and Thirty-Fifth Divisions held the left, from the Aisne to the Butte of Vauquois. At the foot of the butte, also called Vauquois Hill, the Thirty-Fifth was arrayed for battle.

According to Pershing's plan, the First Army's nine in-line divisions were to advance at 5:30 a.m., following an artillery preparation. In industrial age warfare, artillery fire is used to "prepare the terrain" prior to an infantry advance. Lasting from a few minutes to a few hours, an artillery barrage destroys fixed works and equipment, blows holes in barbed wire barriers, and disrupts enemy activity at intersections in his communication lines. Where it doesn't injure or kill the enemy, it puts the fear of God into him.

Planning the Meuse-Argonne Offensive

French General Foch's plan to push the enemy out of his country (American Battle Monuments Commission, *American Armies*, 189). The American First Army is in the south near Verdun.

At the time of attack, "H-hour," the artillery shifts its fire to what's called a "rolling barrage." This is a line of devastation one hundred meters in front of the advancing infantry, which, in this case, is supposed to move at one hundred meters every four minutes. It's rare that the artillerymen can see the line. Therefore, the infantryman is obliged to advance at the set pace. Too slow, he loses the artillery's shock advantage; too fast, he becomes victim to it.

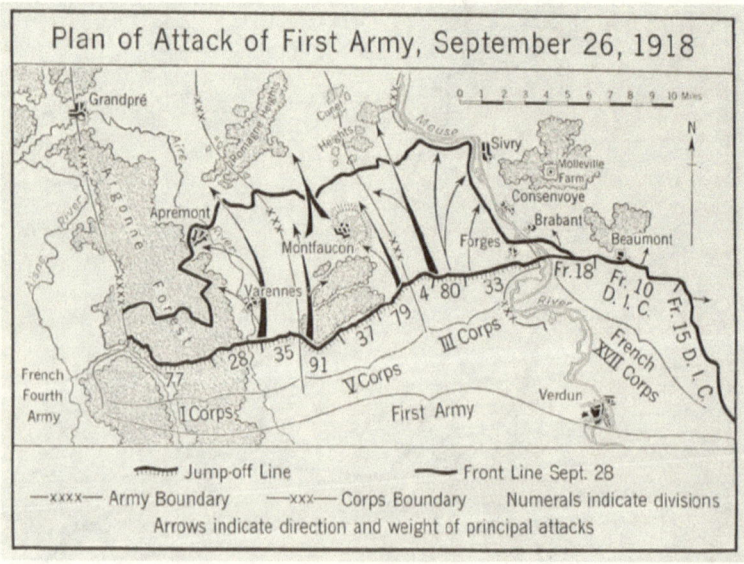

The American sector, September 26, 1918 (ABMC, *American Armies*, 172). Part of First Corps, the Thirty-Fifth Division is positioned east of the Argonne Forest.

Having received the order from First Corps forty-eight hours prior, Thirty-Fifth Division Headquarters issued orders to brigade commanders in the afternoon of September 24. Haterius reproduces the division and brigade "Secret Field Orders," which detail the attack plan (127-144).

The Thirty-Fifth would attack in "column of brigades," meaning each of its two brigades would span the division sector, one behind the other. The Sixty-Ninth Brigade would lead; the Seventieth would follow in support.

Within brigades, regiments were to advance "side by side, each with one battalion in the first line, one in support, and one in reserve" (128). Therefore, the division sector was divided in two. The Sixty-Ninth's 138th Regiment, on the right, would *avoid* Vauquois Hill. On the left, the 137th would take the "V" of Vauquois, a formidable network of trenches, zigzagging from the hill's west flank to the village of Boureuilles [*bor-uhy*] a mile away. This action would cut enemy support to the strategic butte.

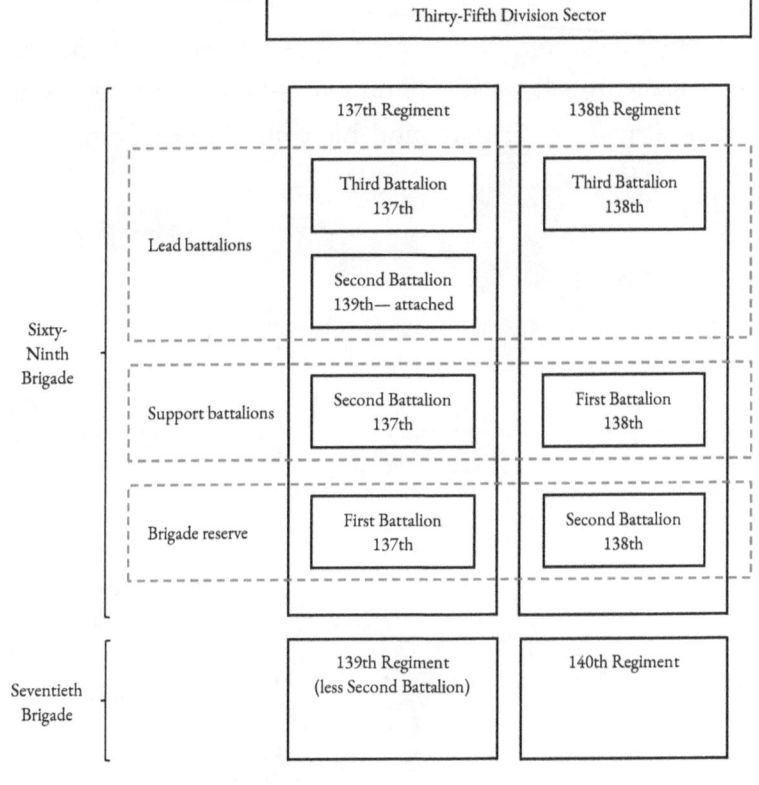

Thirty-Fifth Division attack formation, Meuse-Argonne Offensive.

The 137th Regiment's twelve companies were divided into three battalions. First Battalion, Companies A through D, was assigned to the brigade reserve. Second Battalion, Companies E through H, would support Third Battalion—Companies I through M, which would lead.

From the field orders:

> Parallel of departure for leading battalions—a line approximately 500 meters from the enemy's front-line trenches. (Quoted in Haterius, 139)

In the sector, the stretch of wounded earth between opposing trenches called "no-man's-land" was 500 meters wide. Private B. F. Potts and his comrades of Company M were on its edge.

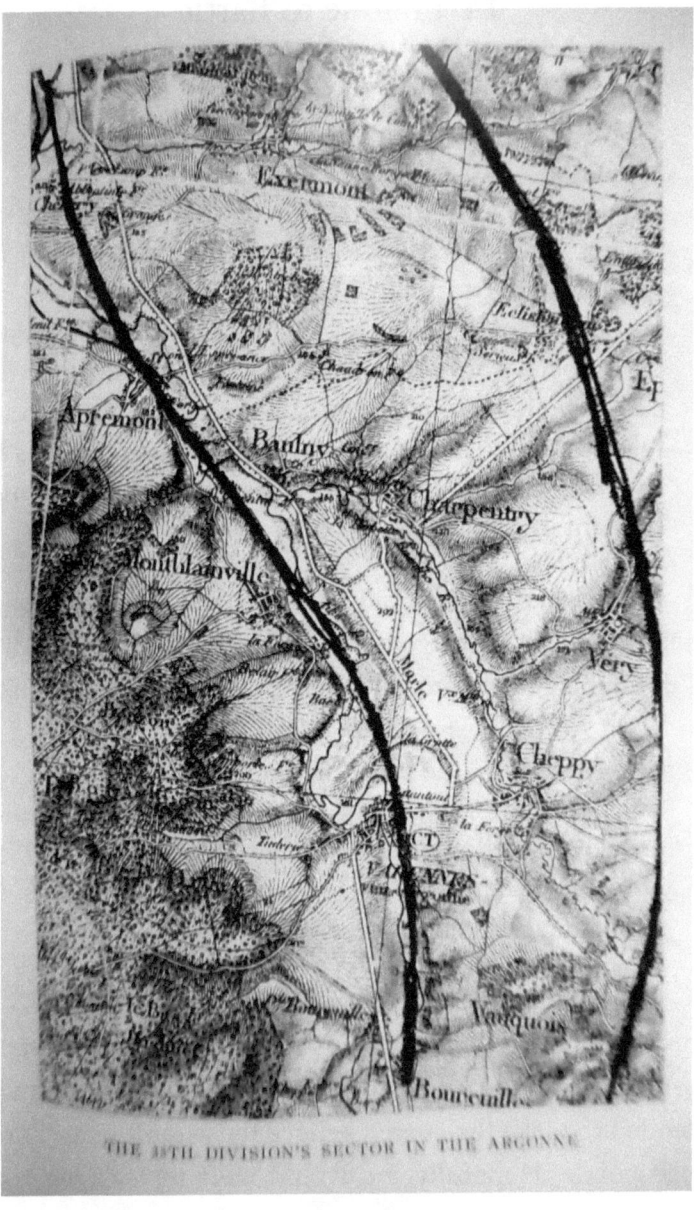

Thirty-Fifth Division sector (Kenamore, facing 176). Note the elevation hatching and the Garamond font of *La carte de l'état-major*.

14 Prelude to Battle

SEPTEMBER 25, 1918

Each infantryman carried his rifle, bayonet, steel helmet and gas mask. He had 250 rounds of rifle ammunition, carried in a belt, and two bandoliers, each one swung over one shoulder and under the other arm. On his back was his combat pack, in his pack carrier. This contained his raincoat, if he was not wearing it, his mess-kit and two days' "iron ration," which usually was two cans of corned beef and six boxes of hard bread. (Kenamore, 88)

Gear issued and packed the afternoon before the battle, Private Potts had a "large hot meal" with his comrades of the 137th Infantry Regiment, crouched in the Hesse Forest (87).

After dark, the infantry moved forward through the woods in approximately the formation they were to employ the following day. *The men lay down among the big guns and tried to sleep.* Each one, according to orders, first loaded and locked his rifle. (88, emphasis mine)

The initial artillery fire began at 11:30 p.m. The guns were aimed east of the Meuse and west of the Argonne Forest, that is, either side of the next day's objective. It was deceptive fire, intended to make the enemy believe the assault would target those points. Hopefully, he would shift his reserve forces there.

"At 2:30 a.m. [on the 26th] all the other artillery concentrated between the Meuse River and the Argonne Forest went into action," writes Kenamore.

> All adjectives fail to give even a fair impression of the awful grandeur of such artillerying. No combination of words is effective. It seemed that for a while the lid of Hell had been pushed back a little space. The long line on either hand leaped into flame, the horizon was lit by the bursting shells, and from the trenches where the enemy had lain so long there rose the many-colored rockets with which he appealed to his guns for succor. What each signal meant I do not know, but they plentifully told the tale of his distress. (89)

A steel chamber holds a brass shell. Inside it, a pin ignites propellant. The confined explosion shoots a projectile and a gout of flame from the 75mm (3 inches) bore. The gun jumps, the earth shudders, a shock wave shatters the air and accompanies a roar that bursts between the ears. Spent, the brass shell slides to the ground with a hallow *shing!* Another round replaces it and, as soon, ignites. Powder fumes permeate the air. Explosions count seconds across unending darkness.

In this infernal night lies our young private, waiting, suspended in time, between sleep and prayer.

15 Taking Vauquois

SEPTEMBER 26, 1918

For the French, it's the Battle of Verdun. For the British, the Somme. For the Americans, the Meuse-Argonne is the superlative battle. The largest battle in US history: 1.2 million American soldiers participated. The longest battle: lasting forty-seven days. The deadliest: 26,277 Americans killed.

The battle ended with the signing of the Armistice, November 11, 1918. It began September 26. For the 137th Infantry Regiment, it began at the "V" of Vauquois. Private Potts, with Company M, was in the lead battalion.

Our battlefield journalists, Clair Kenamore and Carl Haterius, were there.

> At 5:30 a.m. [GMT+1] the infantry went over all along the line. There was no breakfast and little ceremony about it. The lieutenant or sergeant who was leading the platoon, when his watch told him the zero hour was but a few minutes off, would give the order: "Prepare to advance."
>
> The men would crawl out of their foxholes, pick up their raincoats, look to their rifles, and wait. At "H" hour the platoon leader would say: "All right, let's go," and leading the way, he would set his face to the north and move out, his men following. (Kenamore, 90)

> At 5:30 a.m. the signal hour broke, and as the barrage lifted, the commands were given, and the masses of olive drab forms, with helmets adjusted, gas masks in position,

and rifle in hand, rose and scampered up over the top and started for the German positions across the way. (Haterius, 145)

From the battle plan, we know when the artillery's rolling barrage began, as well as its rate of advance. We also know the infantry moved a hundred meters behind it. Therefore, up until 7:40 a.m., when the rolling barrage ceased, we can follow Private Potts's movement across the battlefield.

At H-hour comes the order: "Let's go!" Private Potts crawls out of a shallow hole and heads into no-man's-land. An exploding wall of dirt and debris, the artillery's rolling barrage, precedes him. An orange flash, veiled by dense fog in the predawn dark, reveals for an instant the man on his left and the man on his right and, to his front, grotesque forms in the disheveled land. The ground trembles. The blast pierces the ears. The soldier moves forward.

The effect of our six-hour barrage had been so thorough that the Boche front lines were pulverized beyond recognition. As the boys advanced, they found few if any Germans in the first line trenches; they had gone back into the second and reserve trenches. As the advance reached the second line trenches, the enemy commenced fire upon them, and soon a retaliatory fire of artillery, and machine-gun fire was in operation. (145)

Private Potts's first combat experience is before him, west of Vauquois Hill, east of the town of Boureuilles. Stretched across his path beyond the fog lay four lines of trenches, named Balkans, Serpent, Constantinople, and Enfer [*on-fair*; French for "Hell"].

Company M advances in staggered formation, never presenting a straight-line shot of two men to enemy trenches, with a few meters between each man, to minimize casualties from a single grenade or artillery blast. Ahead, in silhouette against the orange flashes, appears an earthen berm and mangled wire. Drawing no fire from the Balkans trench, the men pass with caution.

Map section (*opposite*): September 26, morning Thirty-Fifth Division, Meuse-Argonne Offensive (ABMC).

One century later, to the minute, we can place Private Benjamin Franklin Potts, with reasonable confidence, in the line between the division left and Hill 253 (*mid-sector*).

Once fairly in the field it became apparent that the going was to be very bad. The autumn frequently brings to that part of France a thick, clinging fog which only a bright sun or a strong wind can disperse. The heaviest fog of the season had descended on the valley of the Aire that morning. At first thought, it appeared that this might be of assistance to the Thirty-fifth, for it would conceal the advancing troops from the waiting machine gunners, but very soon it became apparent that the maintaining of liaison would be most difficult.

Lieut. Bancon, flying over the sector, dropped a message at headquarters at 8:15 a.m., saying: "Impossible to find line. Our sector is a solid white snow-bank of clouds." (Kenamore, 91-92)

Any optimism rising in a soldier's heart on passing the abandoned trench shatters in bursts of machine-gun fire from the next one. Platoon leaders shout orders, incoming artillery blasts the ground, dirt and mud rain down on the soldier, who moves forward in a crouch. *Boom!* A thrown grenade silences the machine gun. Rifles fire in the fog. *Pop! Pop! Tat! Tat! Pop!*

Serpent is littered with gray-clad bodies, still and bleeding. Through the trench the men must trudge. The stench of mud and blood and human waste assails the nose. Up the other side, the soldier looks to his left and right—comrades in the fog, still thick, dull gray before dawn.

The blasts of the rolling barrage more distant, the order cuts through the mist, and Company M advances the line into the next burst of machine-gun fire. Adrenaline pumps in the veins. Legs move without thought. *Tat! Tat! Pop! Boom!*

Constantinople is cleared. Wounds are dressed. Prisoners escorted to the rear. The dead are marked with a rifle, fixed bayonet thrust in the ground; stretcher-bearers are to follow. Again, the order; again, the men advance.

By the time they cleared the last machine gun from their sector of Enfer, the boys of Company M were combat veterans, and the sun had not yet risen over the blanket of fog that covered the battlefield on that first of what would be five days of fighting.

Passing Enfer, Kenamore writes:

> The leading battalion pressed forward, cleaned out the Aden strongpoint, and in the hopeless fog, and with artillery fire which they had met from the first were stopped before the well-constructed defenses of Varennes. Many machine guns opened, and there was no chance to look ahead into the gloom. (127)

Meanwhile, on the right half of the division sector, the 138th Regiment, according to orders, avoided Vauquois Hill, moving around its east flank. This was done to prevent delay in the advancing line. The task of taking the fortified hill and Rossignol Wood behind it was assigned to a battalion of the support regiment.

As our Third Battalion, 137th, cleared the trenches of the "V" of Vauquois, the Second Battalion of the 139th followed close behind. This battalion, once the leading elements had passed Vauquois Hill, veered to the right behind it to attack from the flank.

Never before or afterward did the 35th Division find a place better defended than Vauquois. It was the result of four years intensive work by the Germans. (94)

A high French officer told me their losses there probably totaled 40,000. It was known to be thoroughly mined, to have excavations and tunnels of great length for quick communication and transferal of troops from one point to another. (79)

Whether it was the lengthy bombardment prior to attack, the threat of being surrounded, the hill's reduced strategic importance since the introduction of the airplane, or a combination thereof, when Second Battalion arrived, the Butte of Vauquois was scarcely defended.

Kenamore describes the action in a broad stroke:

[Second Battalion] had methodically cleaned [the dugouts of Vauquois] of all enemy elements, killing or capturing all defenders. (128)

Hoyt gives more detail:

[Second Battalion] had found Vauquois Hill and Bois de Rossignol comparatively easy to handle. In some of the dugouts the moppers-up had found Germans, none of which had shown much fight. They had bombed and cleaned them out as they went along, endeavoring to overlook as few as possible in the fog of impenetrable thickness. (74)

The 139th's Second Battalion rejoined its regiment at 9:30 a.m. south of Varennes. The four-year battle of Vauquois was over.

« *Aux combattants et aux morts de Vauquois* »
Monument to the combatants and the dead of Vauquois, September 24, 1914-September 26, 1918. Photo by the author.

16 Fog of War

SEPTEMBER 26, 1918

> Then [in war] there is a very great difficulty arising from the unreliability of all data. This means that all actions must necessarily be planned and carried out in a more or less uncertain light, which like a fog or moonshine, gives things a somewhat exaggerated and unnatural size and appearance.
> —Clausewitz, *On War*, 1832

Prussian General Carl von Clausewitz used "fog or moonshine" as a metaphor to demonstrate uncertainty in armed conflict. Military leaders and thinkers since have applied the metaphor to the chaos of the battlefield in particular, using the expression "fog of war."

On the morning of September 26, the fog in the Aire Valley was literal as well as figurative. According to Kenamore:

> It was possible to see 40 yards at times, but beyond that the fog shut in like a wall. A squad of men would be observed marching ahead, but a moment later they would entirely disappear, and there would be nothing to see but the opaque gray bank of fog. It was impossible to tell friend from foe 25 yards away. (94-95)

Approaching Varennes, three kilometers (two miles) north of the departure line around 8 a.m., Third Battalion, 137th Regiment, had by now outdistanced the artillery's useful range. The division's Sixtieth Field Artillery Brigade was ordered forward.

But portions of the Sixtieth's planned route, north along *Route Nationale* No. 46, had been destroyed by the retreating enemy. The guns had to be hauled through the mud of the now conquered no-man's-land, some by double teams of horses (one team is six horses), some by platoons of men. Only one battery, which counts four guns, made itself heard that afternoon. The Thirty-Fifth Division would be without artillery support well into the next day.

To make matters worse, across the division boundary on the 137th's left, the Twenty-Eighth Division met stiff resistance in the Argonne Forest. Their advance was slow. What's more, their own artillery, having departed later, was blocked in traffic on the Route Nationale. This left the 137th's left flank open to counterattack by ground troops and artillery fire from the Argonne heights. With troops of the Twenty-Eighth out of range and no artillery to threaten them, enemy machine guns in the sector had nothing to do but fire on the 137th.

> The leading battalion of [the] 137th Infantry had been checked by machine gun and flank artillery fire on the outskirts of the village [Varennes]. Every gray-walled little house, even to the gaunt remains of the town church, seemed to have within a machine gun. (Hoyt, 74)

Here, the regimental commander, Colonel Clad Hamilton, whose headquarters detachment traveled with the battalion, ordered the men to dig in to protect themselves from incoming fire. While waiting for his Second Battalion to come up, Hamilton tried to contact brigade headquarters to get artillery support.

Kenamore devotes a six-page chapter to battlefield communication, its devices, and its failure that day (135-140). Signal flags, flash lamps, and "heliographs" (a system using mirrors) were useless in the fog. Carrier pigeons were confused by the fog, smoke, and artillery fire. The telephone, which depended on a wire connection, was impractical. A frontline signal platoon had got working a wireless set in a shell hole. But, because division headquarters failed to install their own set, they could only listen to the time from the Eiffel Tower.

Map section (*opposite*): September 26, afternoon Thirty-Fifth Division, Meuse-Argonne Offensive (ABMC).

The German *Maschinengewehr 08* fired five hundred rounds a minute at an effective range of two thousand meters (two squares on the map). Also notice the contour lines showing higher elevations west of the Aire, from which German 77mm guns fired down on the 137th before Varennes.

Kenamore also mentions "T. P. S.," which stands for *télégraphie par le sol*. The ground telegraph was invented in 1917 by Frenchman Paul Boucherot. "This is a system of telephoning without wires, using the ground as a conducting medium. It is most successful for distances up to a few miles" (136-137). T. P. S. seems to have been also ineffective.

> Runners were the only means left, and they had almost no landmarks to guide them through the fog and smoke. (137)

We have previously assumed that Private Potts was selected to be a runner. In the present situation, a commander, having exhausted other more immediate means at his disposal, might resort to this method of communication.

Scrawling in a notepad, the commander tears the sheet and thrusts it into the runner's hands.

"Potts, take this message to brigade. Tell them we need artillery now—Go!"

Off he goes, message secured in a pocket, rifle in hand, chin strap fastened tight. As he moves down the slopes south of Varennes, Private Potts dodges machine-gun fire and artillery shells. Brigade headquarters' last known position is at Mamelon Blanc, a hilltop four kilometers (2.5 miles) away on the other side of Vauquois Hill.

While the 137th was stalled before Varennes, the support regiment, the 139th, moved up, passing the town on the east, to continue the advance. Farther to the right, the 138th took

Cheppy around 9 a.m. Without artillery support, the 344th Tank Battalion, of the First Tank Brigade, came to their aid. The tank brigade commander came up on foot to see how the tanks were performing. Thirty-two-year-old Lieutenant Colonel George Patton was hit by a machine gunner's bullet. He didn't sit comfortably for some weeks thereafter.

Gasping for breath, Private Potts slows to a walk as he approaches a group of men and horses dragging a big gun through mud.

"Pull, pull, pull!" says one man at the front of a line of men on a rope. The gun's wheels turn out of a depression, gaining several feet.

The lead man turns to inspect progress. "Sergeant, get some branches to put under the wheels."

"Yes, sir," says the sergeant. "Let's trim that tree, men!"

Potts calls out, "Excuse me, sir, I'm looking for the Sixty-Ninth Brigade Headquarters."

The officer steps forward, removing round-rimmed spectacles to wipe sweat from his brow. His straight nose forms a perfect triangle.

"There's a road a mile that way," he says, throwing an arm eastward. "They'll be somewhere along there."

"Thank you, sir, and good luck!" says Potts, as he breaks into a trot through the mud.

> The failure of liaison and all mechanical means of communication cost the lives of many brave men in the front lines in the course of the battle.... Runners would be dispatched. If they were not killed or wounded en route, they probably would find the agile brigade headquarters had moved from the shell hole in which it had last been seen, and there would be no one there to tell where it was gone. The search for the headquarters would continue while the battery or machine gun nest would continue to take its toll of American lives. (Kenamore, 137)

If the runner found headquarters and managed the return journey, the response he carried would have informed the regimental commander the artillery was not in position. In either case, by 10:30 a.m., the 137th's Second Battalion came in line with the Third. As the fog cleared, fire from the flank became more intense. If troops are taking fire, they may as well be taking ground too. The assault on Varennes was accomplished without artillery support.

> Beyond Varennes was situated what was known as the "Grotto," a wooded hill surmounted by an ancient chapel and shrine. Numerous machine-guns were pivoted here, and a battery of "seventy-sevens" [German 77mm artillery guns] made it a "strong point" of no mean calibre. The Grotto was taken by noon of the 26th by the Second and Third Battalions. (Haterius, 146)

By 4:00 p.m., the Thirty-Fifth Division halted along a line five kilometers from the morning's parallel of departure. Though, due to the confusion of the day, the units were well mixed, their general positions are recorded as follows: Having passed ahead, the 139th held the line one kilometer south of Charpentry. East of Buanthe Creek, the 138th was at the top of the hill northwest of Véry, the 140th to its south. The 137th dug in north of Varennes.

As night falls on the Aire Valley, Private B. F. Potts is overwhelmed by a profound sense of fatigue. He hasn't eaten since yesterday; congestion on the roads and continued shelling prevent food from coming up so far. His canteen is empty; the retreating enemy is known to poison water points behind it. In the dark, he would like to lie down and sleep, despite falling artillery, but he is denied even that. Fog of war be damned, there is still work to do.

> The sleepless runners pounded away on the eternal task of trying to find in the darkness an unknown Colonel and deliver to him a message from a Brigadier-General who would assuredly have moved before the runner returned. (Kenamore, 141)

17 Night Attack

September 27, 1918

The confusion that began in the fog the morning before continued through the next day. Around 3:00 a.m., the 137th Regiment, now behind the 139th, received orders to support the lead regiment in its morning attack. The attack was to begin at 8:30, after a three-hour artillery barrage. The 137th received a new order some while later, giving 5:30 as the hour of attack, after only a five-minute barrage. Around 5 a.m., a third order put H-hour at 6:30; the barrage to last one-hour.

The following cry might have been heard, bounding in the darkness between the slopes on either side of Buanthe Creek:

"Let him lie in an artillery shower all night if you must, but do not disturb a soldier's sleep, sir, with your orders that change from one minute to the next!"

Units had got mixed in the fog the first morning, and continued shelling prevented any reorganization. So, at this point, Private Potts could have been anywhere in the division sector. There are reported cases where an individual, a detachment, or an entire battalion went beyond the front line shown on the map. Nevertheless, not having any anecdotes from Grandpa Ben saying he had been too far forward, we assume he was behind the limit of advance.

At 5:30, the men of the 137th heard rifle shots and the distinct sound of American machine guns. The noise came from the front but to their right, where the 140th Regiment had not received the third order. More worrying to their ears was what they didn't hear. While the German artillery kept up through the night and now increased in intensity, their own artillery, which was to prepare the terrain for the attack, was silent.

Still no barrage at 6:30, the 137th prepared to move forward behind the 139th. They waited. At seven o'clock, enemy artillery increased to their fore. Finally, lieutenants and sergeants passed an order down the line: "Prepare to advance!"

"We're ready, sir. Let us at those damn guns!"

Still they waited. Rain clouds gathered overhead.

This confusion of orders, resulting from a failure of communication, is a typical battlefield scenario. In the modern military, enlisted personnel and officers alike use a special term for it: "cluster," in its short form. Although it's outside the scope of this narrative, Kenamore, in four pages, recounts the episode from the brigade and division commanders' perspective (148-151).

To summarize pertinent events: Unknown to the waiting troops, the 139th's regimental commander sent a message by runner to the brigade at 6:30, saying he was ready to attack as soon as he had artillery. With no reply and no artillery at 7:00, the commander advanced the regiment anyway.

> His formation caught the full fire of the enemy artillery and machine guns. Ristine [139th commander] was able to advance, but as he saw the swaths the opposing fire was making in his ranks, he decided the price was too heavy. He halted his regiment, ordered the

men to dig in, and sent a message to brigade headquarters that he could not advance further without artillery support. (Kenamore, 151)

Behind the 139th, the 137th Regiment and, to the right, the remainder of the Thirty-Fifth Division waited throughout the day under clouds that threatened rain and a shower of enemy shells that threatened an end to their suffering.

Kenamore cites a message to the Thirty-Fifth Division commander, General Traub, from General Pershing:

> He expects the 35th Division to move forward. He is not satisfied with the Division being stopped by machine gun nests here and there. He expects the Division to move forward now in accordance to orders. (Quoted in Kenamore, 154)

We might imagine the impact of the curt message on the division general, not from his corps commander but from the next higher—the army commander himself. The message, received at 4:30 p.m., lit a fire that spread down the chain of command.

Map section (*opposite*): September 27 Thirty-Fifth Division, Meuse-Argonne Offensive (ABMC).

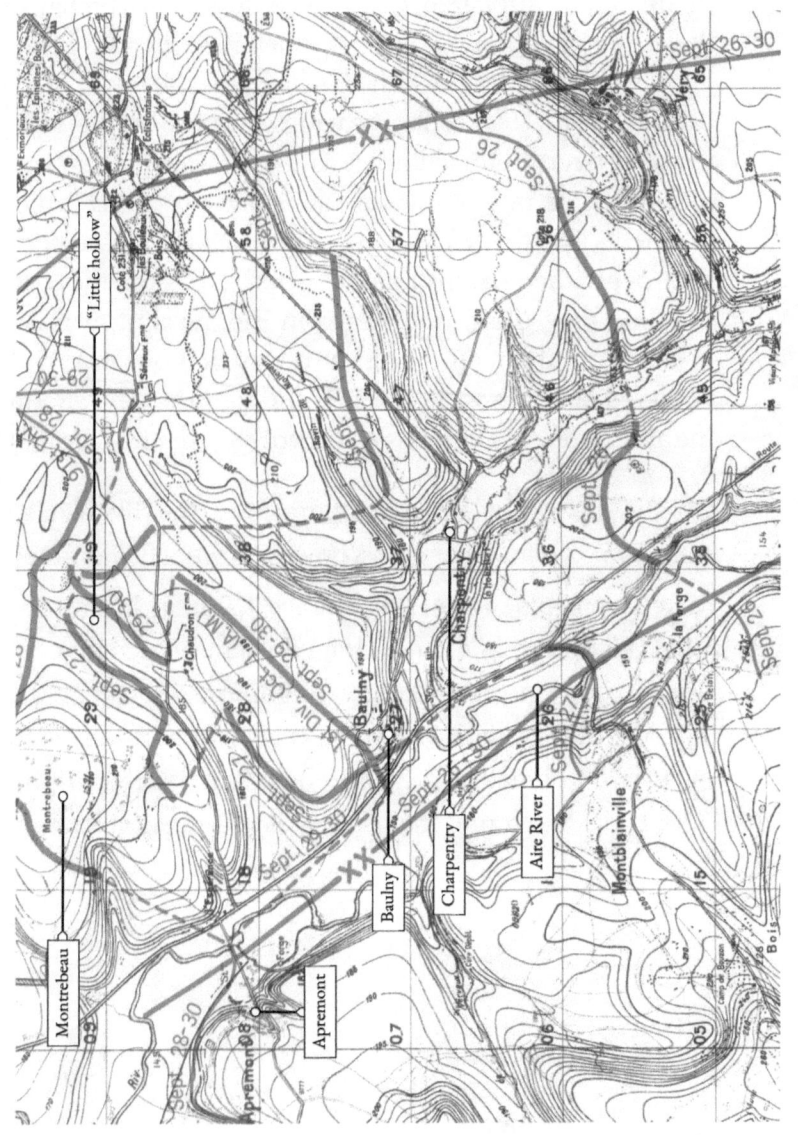

> At 5:30 [p.m.] the division stood upon its feet amidst its dead, and prepared to advance, to show whether it was as good a fighting outfit as it believed it was.
> ... The 139th came out of its foxholes like war dogs off the leash. They took a singeing fire full in the face, charged over the machine guns and stamped them out like nests of rats and, with assistance of other units [elements of the 137th and 138th], had taken both Charpentry and Baulny before stopping to count the cost. The line they could not breach in the morning was no weaker. It did not crumble. But it was as if our men had gathered strength while waiting through the day, and in the afternoon the Germans could not stop them. (155-156)

On the right, the 140th, supported by the 138th, also advanced at 5:30 p.m. Their gains, however, were not as great.

Mixed elements of the 139th and the 137th, including our Third Battalion, dug in after midnight. The lead element lay "in a little hallow" north of Baulny (Kenamore, 158). With the lagging Twenty-Eighth Division, on their left, and the 140th Regiment two kilometers (1.24 miles) behind, on their right, the 137th and 139th found themselves defending a salient.

18 Montrebeau Wood

SEPTEMBER 28, 1918

The sun rose, unseen. A cold, drizzling rain fell from a close sky. On the slopes of the hollow north of Baulny, men of the 137th and 139th Regiments lay, soaking wet, chilled to the bone. Sleep was impossible with the cold, the damp, and the night's steady shelling.

A hundred meters northwest of the hollow rose a gentle hill, leading up to a line of trees: the wood of Montrebeau [*mon-tra-boh*; "showing beauty"]. As the sky lightened from its darkest black, the shelling increased, and a wave of gray-clad soldiers broke from the wood, rushing down the hill. The enemy skirmish line was repulsed with machine-gun and rifle fire. So began the Thirty-Fifth Infantry Division's third day of battle.

The day's orders were to advance through Montrebeau Wood. The attack would begin at 6:30 a.m. Today, the infantrymen would have support from their artillery, though it would never be as heavy as the first morning.

> All the glory was gone out of the war, with the glitter and pageantry of the first day's successes, but they went ahead. They were not the dashing lads who went over the top two days before, but they were veterans of battle, hardened soldiers who no longer had any delusions about a soldier's life. (Kenamore, 178)

They advanced through strafing machine-gun fire from the woods ahead. Haterius quotes a French officer, who observed the action: "Those d— Americans have no sense; they know not when to stop; they go against machine-gun fire barehanded" (146). By morning's end, the intermingled 137th and 139th gained 500 meters and dug in before Montrebeau Wood.

> Montrebeau Wood was a thick tangle of trees and underbrush about the size of a square kilometer. It contains, I should say on a guess, 240 acres. There were many lines and systems of barbed wire entanglements thrown through it. The Americans had to cut paths through this wire. The Germans had trails already made, which they knew, but it was difficult and dangerous for our men to find them. (Kenamore, 178-179)

Through the woods and machine-gun nests and sniper fire, the men fought in the afternoon. By dark, they held a line on its northern edge.

On the division right, the 140th launched the day's attack an hour earlier. Orders to the commander were "to take his regiment forward with all speed to protect the flank of the troops on his left [the 137th and 139th]" (179). The regiment pushed through relentless artillery fire, being more exposed as they advanced over the northern, enemy-facing slopes. In the evening, they dug in just north of the hollow, which had been occupied by their division comrades on the left the previous night.

Map section (*opposite*): September 28
Thirty-Fifth Division, Meuse-Argonne Offensive (ABMC).

Tonight, the Thirty-Fifth Division defended a cohesive front on the north edge of Montrebeau Wood, from its western slopes to 500 meters northwest of Sérieux Farm, where the Thirty-Fifth connected to the Ninety-First Division on its right. Furthermore, on its left, the Twenty-Eighth Division made advances in the day, taking Apremont, near the western division boundary. There was, though, a gap in the Thirty-Fifth's sector between it and the Twenty-Eighth.

19 Encounter at Creek's Edge

When I asked Grandpa Ben if he killed anyone, this is what he said: They had just been in action and his best friend had been killed that day and he was very upset. As he left the area, he was walking through the woods and came up behind a German soldier, eating his lunch as he was sitting on a rock next to a stream. Grandpa said he tried to turn to go in a different direction away from the soldier but stepped on a stick or leaves and made noise, which alerted the German to his presence. The German soldier reached for his rifle, so, Grandpa said, he had no choice and shot the soldier. Then Grandpa told me something I'll never forget: "He fell forward into the creek, and I never did see that boy again."

—*Bruce Potts*

20 Charge to Exermont

September 29, 1918

In war, a "casualty" is a soldier who suffers any condition that puts him or her out of action, which includes being killed as well as wounded, whether in battle or by accident. During the four days in which the Thirty-Fifth Division advanced the line, it suffered 8,023 casualties (Kenamore, 240). The fourth day of fighting would be its bloodiest day.

So many casualties would reduce a full-strength division by one quarter. But, since the division began the battle undermanned, its four infantry regiments were reduced to half strength (241).

The division also went into battle with half the quota of officers for the troop count. So, the high casualty rate put a strain on the leadership. Even with staff officers converted to line officers, by the previous day some battalions were commanded by lieutenants.

A thinning olive drab line held back the enemy the morning of the 29th. A heavy rain fell on Montrebeau Wood. Beneath the dense canopy, darkness pervaded, lit up by occasional enemy artillery fire. The day's orders were to attack at 5:30 a.m. The objective: Exermont.

Map section (*opposite*): September 29 Thirty-Fifth Division, Meuse-Argonne Offensive (ABMC).

The village of Exermont lay in a ravine running east-west across the division sector. Of the town, Kenamore writes, "Tolerably well placed for defense . . ., it was ringed three-quarters of the way round with cannon and machine guns" (205).

What's more, from Hill 240 behind the town came much of the artillery fire that had so devastated the ranks in preceding days. Today, the troops would be in range of machine-gun fire from those heights as well.

The plan for the 137th was to attack in two waves. Major Kalloch, who had been the division intelligence officer the evening before, would lead the first wave. The units were so mixed on the division left we can no longer speak of battalions. The officers just rounded up what men they could find to carry out the mission.

Major Kalloch put 125 men "mostly of the 137th" into an attack formation (205). At 5:30 a.m., he waited for the artillery barrage promised by division orders. Four minutes later, the major led the men from the concealment of Montrebeau Wood without the friendly barrage.

Kalloch advanced through heavy artillery and machine-gun fire. As the men would destroy one machine-gun nest, other enemy gun crews were setting up on both sides of their skirmish line. Taking out these nests one after another, Kalloch and his men reached the ravine west of Exermont, loses mounting. The major ordered the men to dig in.

There was no sign anywhere of the supporting wave Col. Hamilton [137th commander] was to bring out, so Kalloch sent two runners, one a few minutes behind the other, to say that he could go no farther without support. (206)

When the second wave, led by Major O'Connor under Colonel Hamilton's orders, emerged from Montrebeau Wood, it was full daylight. O'Connor's troops took artillery and machine-gun fire from three sides.

> The men were willing and brave, but much disorganized, largely, I suspect, through their great physical weariness. The officers were unable to maneuver them. When they reached the top of the rise and got the full force of the fire, they seemed just to fade back into the woods. (207)

At eight o'clock, with more enemy machine guns filtering down the slope before his line and without reinforcements of his own, Major Kalloch was forced to retire with his troops from Exermont.

Later in the morning, larger elements of the 139th, on the division left, and the 140th, on the right, were successful in an assault on the village. Kenamore describes the charge in the face of enemy fire:

> In the stunning, dumbing gust of war, the men sensed with their physical bodies rather than their minds, that death was pouring past them in a flood. As if they were walking forward through a driving hailstorm they turned their faces to leeward and, leaning forward against the blast, pushed ahead with the point of shoulder offered to the gale. (209)

They took the village and held a line on the southern slope of Hill 240. But reinforcements were not forthcoming, and communication was difficult with commanders to the rear. The 140th commander wasn't even aware that part of his regiment had made it so far forward.

When General Traub came up around eleven o'clock to assess the situation, he found the division strength much depleted, its units disorganized. In a message to First Corps Headquarters, the general wrote:

> Regret to report that this Division cannot advance beyond crest south of Exermont. It is thoroughly disorganized through loss of officers and many casualties, for which cannot give estimate, owing to intermingling of units. Recommend it be withdrawn for reorganization and be replaced promptly by other troops in order that the advance may be continued. (Quoted in Kenamore, 217)

Soon after, the division's 110th Engineer Regiment received orders to construct a defensive line below the ridge running northeast from Baulny. Forward units were then ordered to withdraw to that line. The order to withdraw was delivered by runner.

"Where's Private Potts?"

"Here, sir!"

"This message is for Colonel Hamilton, 137th, in Montrebeau Wood. His regiment is to cover the withdraw of troops from Exermont before pulling back. If the colonel doesn't get the word A.S.A.P., our boys from Exermont will be sitting ducks. Do you understand?"

Potts, who leapt from the shell hole at "A.S.A.P.," shouts, "Understood, sir!" over a shoulder.

Where any-sized formation of men must spread itself out to advance through enemy fire as well as arrive in force at the objective, a lone man chooses a narrow path and not necessarily the most direct route to the destination. He negotiates the terrain, dodging enemy fire, exposing himself as little as possible, and taking advantage of battlefield distractions.

Message delivered, the messenger may have withdrawn with the troops. A "withdraw" is a tactical movement where one-half a unit—say, a six-man team—fires toward the enemy's position to keep their heads down (this is called "suppressive fire"), while another team moves back several yards. Then, the second team lays down suppressive fire, while the first team moves back. By this leapfrog action, the unit may cede ground without overexposing itself to enemy fire.

Far enough removed from the German line, Private Potts and the ragtag platoon he accompanies hasten south. A hill rises to one side. Below its crest, a man crouches at the edge of a shell hole, looking through field glasses to the north, steel helmet cocked back. Another soldier adjusts dials on a field telephone, while a third approaches from the south and hops into the hole with a spool, wire trailing.

Potts hollers, "Hey, fellows!"

The crouching man lowers the field glasses, revealing round-rimmed spectacles and a triangle nose.

"We're falling back to Chaudron Farm, sir. The Germans'll be here any minute."

The hole's occupants jump into activity, gathering equipment. The officer snaps orders while stowing the field glasses in a pack. Potts hurries on.

That night, with the remains of four infantry regiments, the 110th Engineers defended the prepared line against counterattack. Although the officers and men didn't know it yet, the Thirty-Fifth Infantry Division had made its last advance of the Great War.

21 Clyde Brake Boards the *Leviathan*

September 29, 1918

In 1913, the German-owned Hamburg America Line launched a series of three steamships, each one larger than its predecessor. The first, the *Imperator*, outsized the *Titanic*, which sank in the North Atlantic the year before. The *Vaterland* ("Fatherland" in German) was the second. It measured 950 feet in length and carried 54,282 tons of cargo. Third in the series, the *Bismarck* carried 2,000 tons more and was six feet longer (Smith, *Trans-Atlantic Passenger Ships*, 257).

The *Vaterland*, 1914.

At the outbreak of war, the *Imperator* was at port in Hamburg, as was the *Bismarck*, not yet fitted out. The *Vaterland* was moored at Hoboken, New Jersey.

In the morning of April 6, 1917, the day the US declared war on the German Empire, American troops seized the *Vaterland* at its mooring in the Hoboken harbor. Within weeks, the ship was pressed into service as a troop transport, renamed the *Leviathan*.

Clyde Brake Potts (*opposite*) in uniform wearing campaign hat, 1918.

In regulation use from as early as the 1870s, the campaign hat was standard issue to US Army soldiers throughout the Great War. But its stiff, broad brim and four-cornered "Montana peak" made the felt headgear difficult to store when not needed. Upon entry into the war, the US Army adopted the narrow, creased cap from the French. The *bonnet de police*, made of soft cloth, could be folded over a belt.

In 1917 and early 1918, the cap was issued in France and, so, came to be known as the "overseas cap." By mid-1918, the men exchanged their campaign hats for overseas caps at the Stateside port of embarkation. Therefore, in the photo, Uncle Clyde, who was drafted in late 1918, must be in the US, either at Camp Wadsworth, South Carolina, or at Camp Merritt, New York.

At first the troops disdained the new head cover. Though, as it was issued only to soldiers serving in Europe, the overseas cap, worn cocked to one side, became a symbol in which returning troops took pride.

September 29, 1918, while his brothers Roy Albert and Benjamin Franklin fought in the Somme and the Meuse, Private Clyde Brake Potts, Company G, Fifty-Seventh Pioneer Infantry, boarded the *Leviathan* at Hoboken, New Jersey, bound for France.

Clyde Brake Potts, the *Leviathan*. Where his brothers listed their father's name as next of kin, the youngest boy gave Mrs. Ellen Potts, mother.

22 The Engineers' Line

SEPTEMBER 30, 1918

This morning what was left of the Thirty-Fifth Division lay in defensive positions built by the 110th Engineers the previous day. These were a long series of short, shallow trenches, not man-height but deeper than a foxhole, from which the troops might repulse a counterattack. The division would lie here throughout the day, under continuing shell fire.

During the first three days of the advance, the 110th Engineer Regiment's job was to repair roads for horse-drawn vehicles, which brought ammunition, rations, and equipment from the rear. Behind the front lines, the engineers filled a noncombat role.

At 10:00 p.m. September 28, by order of General Traub, the 110th Engineers were made division reserve, therefore, combatants, and equipped with rifles, ammunition, and grenades.

Map section (*opposite*): September 30 Thirty-Fifth Division, Meuse-Argonne Offensive (ABMC).

The next day, under constant artillery fire, the engineers dug two miles of trenches from Baulny to Sérieux Farm. When the digging was done, they dropped into the trenches, exchanged shovels for rifles, and pointed them north. Throughout the afternoon and evening of the 29th, as the exhausted infantrymen arrived from Exermont and Montrebeau Wood, the engineer officers placed them in the line.

Kenamore calls September 30 "a desperate day" (235). The few remaining officers tried to organize the line for defense, but in some parts of the trenches, the troops were too bunched up: one artillery shell could take out several men. In other parts, they were too thin: machine gunners held sections without riflemen in support. Fatigued, hungry, thirsty, sleep-deprived, many suffering from dysentery, the men had reached the physical limit of functioning.

> Despite all the men could do to fulfill the dictates of duty, the supreme weariness of the last four days of fighting, now entering on the fifth, was not to be easily triumphed over. What they did was by sheer will, for bodies were numb and reacted slowly to thoughts that would drive them. (Hoyt, 119)

That day, three counterattacks were launched on the trenches by a determined enemy. Three counterattacks were repulsed. With the strength of will left in them, the men of the Thirty-Fifth held the engineers' line.

23 Relieved

OCTOBER 1, 1918

At 3 a.m., the Thirty-Fifth Infantry was the fourth of Pershing's nine frontline divisions to be relieved.

The troops of the First Infantry Division, in country since June 1917, were veterans of the battles of Cantigny, Soissons, and Saint-Mihiel. When they pressed the attack four days later, they fought for eight days to reach the other side of Fléville, a mile northwest of Exermont.

Meanwhile, the battle-weary Thirty-Fifth filed back to Cheppy. From there, they marched south then east, to Vavincourt, where they rested from October 6 to 11.

> The days [at Vavincourt] were not without their drills, their policing, and all that is a part of the camp routine. The soldier had heard much of the rest camps, where men wined and dined after they had suffered heavy fighting.
> The rest camp, it was found, was another army chimera. Reveille, retreat, drill, and a repetition of all those things they had done over and over again for nearly a year and a half, was what greeted them daily. Vin rouge and bad beer they had, if that would be called wining; bully-beef and beans they had, if that could be called dining. The rest camp made the soldier long for the battle. (Hoyt, 123)

Marching south (Hoyt, 117).

Rested and reequipped, the Thirty-Fifth marched again east to the Sommedieue sector, a quiet stretch of front south of Verdun. There, it relieved a French division in the trenches October 14. In the sector, the 137th Regiment took over the Bouée subsector on the division right.

> In the Sommedieue sector, there was little doing, although it was, generally speaking, much livelier than the old days in the Vosges. All four regiments were in the line, each having two battalions in the line and one in support. (Kenamore, 246)

> It was while on this sector the first seven-days furloughs were granted to the men. Grenoble, yet uninvaded by Americans, was the first furlough area thrown open to the Thirty-fifth or other organizations of the A. E. F. The French met the train at the depot with flags, bands and cheers. Pretty girls blew kisses from

their finger tips and old women waved and wiped away the tears. There were twelve hundred men of the division who tasted again of the sweetmeats of civilization. They were given good rooms in good hotels, good meals at the best eating houses, and with no cost to themselves. They answered to no call except their own whims, went where they pleased in the city, and were treated as guests. (Hoyt, 127)

These "seven-days furloughs" are important for an upcoming war story. If the men are getting leave, the officers are taking advantage of time off as well. When a commanding officer is off duty, remaining officers rotate through the position of "duty officer" to handle day-to-day responsibilities.

The Thirty-Fifth would leave the Sommedieue sector on November 6, marching to Chaumont-sur-Aire before going back to the area of Saint-Mihiel November 10.

PART THREE

HOMEWARD

24 Roy Albert Buried Alive!

OCTOBER 7, 1918

The injury that forced Uncle Roy into the field hospital was he was near the spot where a shell landed and was buried under dirt. He was rescued only because his hand was aboveground, and someone saw it moving and dug him out.

—Bruce Potts

For all the fuss over our ancestor Benjamin Franklin Potts, we mustn't ignore his older brother Roy Albert. Not only did Uncle Roy precede Ben to Camp Gordon by nine months, he shipped to France in May 1918, fought in the Somme, was wounded in battle, and still didn't get home until April the next year, a month before Ben's homecoming.

Here, then, is the story of Roy Albert Potts. I regret its brevity and that I never knew Great Uncle Roy.

At twenty-four, Roy Albert Potts was inducted into military service September 21, 1917, at the Houston County Courthouse. The next day, he entrained to Camp Gordon, Georgia, for basic training. He joined the Thirtieth Infantry Division in October at Camp Sevier, South Carolina. As a member of Company K, 117th Infantry Regiment, Roy Albert embarked, on May 11, aboard the *Anselm*, part of a convoy headed for Liverpool, England.

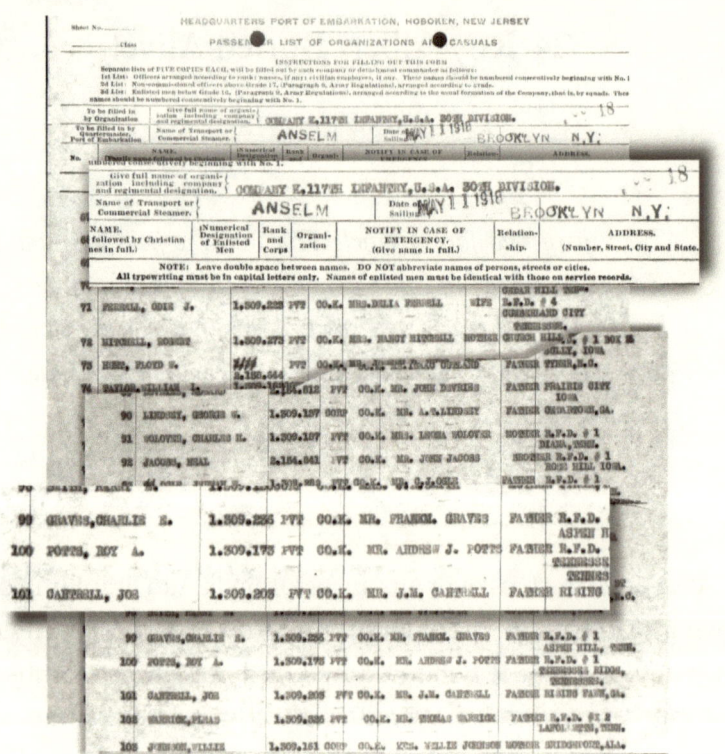

Roy Albert Potts, the *Anselm*.

In France, the Thirtieth Division fought under British command in the Somme Offensive. On October 6, the division relieved the Australian Fifth Division and took command of a sector that included the town of Montbrehain. In difficult fighting the previous day, the Australians had taken Montbrehain but left a salient on the division left.

The British Fourth Army, under which the Thirtieth Division served, had issued orders for a general attack to begin October 8. To straighten the line of departure, the Thirtieth Division commander ordered the salient reduced in a preliminary operation the day before. The division's 117th Regiment was in the line before the salient.

The American Battle Monuments Commission published a series of books in 1944, summarizing the operations of each division in World War I. In the volume concerning the Thirtieth Division, operations down to company level are noted. The following excerpt contains the only mentions of the 117th Infantry Regiment's Company K, which was part of Third Battalion.

> [October 7, 1918, 5:15 a.m.] The 3d Battalion, 117th Infantry, attacked with Companies M, L and I in line from right to left, and Company K in close support. . . . Strong resistance was encountered at once, but Company M gained its objective and established liaison with the 118th Infantry [on its right]. Companies L and I received heavy fire from the vicinity of Bois de la Palette, Genève and Ponchaux [villages near Beaurevoir, *map inset, upper left*]. The [friendly] artillery did not completely cover the left of the line and the British did not advance on that flank. Elements of the center reached the objective, but the left detachments made only a small gain. At 6:40 a.m. detachments of Company K were sent in to fill the gap which had developed between Companies L and I. (ABMC, *30th Division*, 21-22)

Although Roy Albert could have been buried by the fallout from an artillery shell in fighting on any number of days before or after, the fight to reduce the salient is one in which we have a historical document noting Company K's participation. Furthermore, according to statistics given by the American Battle Monuments Commission (10, 35), the

117th took a large proportion of their wounded casualties in the period October 3-14. This, plus the excerpt's mention of heavy artillery on the left of the salient fight, makes October 7 a likely date for the incident.

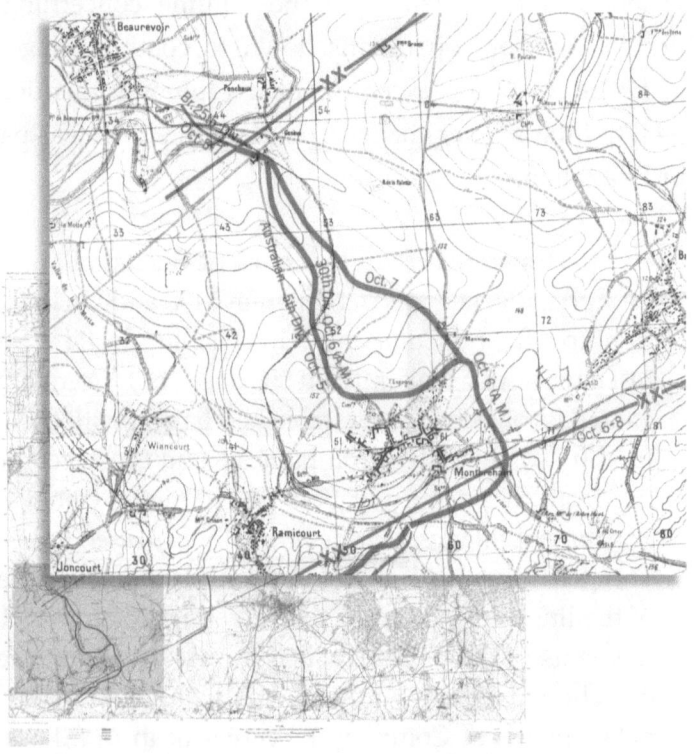

Map: *30th Division, Somme Offensive, October 3-22, 1918* (ABMC, 1938). Inset: Enlargement showing the salient reduced October 7.

After being pulled from an early grave, Roy Albert was taken to a field hospital. Sometime later, at Rembercourt, 125 miles to the southeast, Private Benjamin Franklin Potts received word that his brother Roy was killed in action.

25 Nightmare at Sea

SEPTEMBER 29-OCTOBER 7, 1918

Clyde Brake Potts, on September 5, followed his two older brothers' steps to the Houston County Courthouse. There, he took the oaths of an enlisted man in the United States Army. Unlike his brothers, who received military training at Camp Gordon before going overseas to combat the enemy, Clyde Brake neither went to Camp Gordon nor received military training. Fortunately, he didn't see combat either. His voyage to France, however, was a nightmare.

The Fifty-Seventh Pioneer Infantry Regiment was organized in February 1918 at Camp Wadsworth, South Carolina. It was made up of 500 officers and men from the Vermont National Guard. After six months of training, they were due to ship out in September.

To bring the unit up to strength, twenty-five hundred Tennessee draftees were assigned to the Fifty-Seventh on September 12. Private Clyde Brake Potts became a member of Company G, which was part of Second Battalion. Eleven days later, time enough for the newcomers to be equipped and vaccinated, the regiment entrained to Camp Merritt outside of Hoboken to prepare for their overseas journey.

In a Vermont newspaper article, published in 1920, the regiment's personnel adjutant, Major E. W. Gibson, recounts the trans-Atlantic voyage. Describing the march from Camp Merritt down to the docks, where ferries waited to take them to the *Leviathan*, Gibson writes:

The second and third battalions marched out from their barracks about 1 a.m. on the morning of the 29th of September. We had proceeded but a short distance when it was discovered that men were falling out of ranks, unable to keep up. . . . The column was halted, the camp surgeon was summoned. ("Tells of Horrible Conditions on Giant Troop Ship Leviathan," *Brattleboro (VT) Daily Reformer*, February 12, 1920)

The surgeon's diagnosis: Spanish flu.

The 1918 Spanish influenza pandemic became the deadliest ever recorded. Caused by the H1N1 influenza virus, it was named after the country that seemed to have been hardest hit. But this was an effect of censorship. Warring nations suppressed news reports about the virus's impact at home. Neutral Spain did not.

Indifferent to international borders, Spanish flu circled the globe in waves, from 1918 through 1920, infecting a third of the world's population. With a mortality rate of at least ten percent, it killed up to one hundred million—five percent of humans at the time.

Its symptoms were like any flu: fever, aching joints, nausea, and diarrhea. Unlike most flu viruses, which kill more infants and elderly, Spanish flu killed more otherwise healthy adults. Many victims developed pneumonia. Often, prior to death, a victim turned blue, suffocating as the lungs filled with blood.

Despite a military organization's dependence on strict adherence to orders, leaders are encouraged to analyze a developing situation, and if necessary, disobey an order. In that case, the leader takes responsibility for subsequent outcomes, whether good or bad—the results of his or her "command decision."

In the Fifty-Seventh's case, while common sense might have dictated immediate quarantine, no operating order countermanded the regiment's orders to embark. An argument could be made that the commander failed to make a command decision. Be that as it may, the sick were carried back to the camp hospital, and the Fifty-Seventh Pioneers boarded the *Leviathan* as ordered.

The *Leviathan* was not only the largest ship on the seas, it was also the fastest. At twenty-four knots, it would cross the Atlantic in eight days. German U-boats, much slower, would have to be in its path to fire on it. No need for a warship escort, the *Leviathan* steamed out of New York's Lower Bay and set out across the Atlantic Ocean alone.

Although a similar flu outbreak aboard the *President Grant* claimed more lives, Alfred W. Crosby uses the *Leviathan*'s September 29 voyage in *America's Forgotten Pandemic: The Influenza of 1918*, because "the *Leviathan*'s records are more complete, and her story is gruesome enough to illustrate what the very worst was like" (126).

Quarters were cramped. The vessel carried 6,800 passengers as a peacetime cruise liner. As a troop transport, its bunks were stacked four high. With the Fifty-Seventh's 3,400 men, an additional 6,000 troops (mostly draftees), 2,000 crew, and 200 army nurses, total personnel aboard the *Leviathan* approached 12,000.

By the time the men found their bunks, more were falling ill. The nurses, on their way to army hospitals in France, went to work, assisting the ship's overwhelmed hospital staff. By the evening of the 30th, seven hundred flu cases spilled out of sick bay. One man was already dead.

In the news article, Gibson cites an official report from the medical officer, which describes the scene on the night of September 30:

> Pools of blood, from the severe nasal hemorrhages of many patients, were scattered throughout the compartments, and the attendants were powerless to escape tracking through this mess, because of the narrow passages between the bunks. Everyone called for water and lemons and oranges. A plentiful supply enabled their desire to be gratified. But within a few minutes of the first distribution of fruit, the skins and pulp were added to the blood and vomitus upon the deck. The decks became wet and slippery; the filth clung to the clothing of the attendants; groans and cries of the terrified sick added to the confusion of the applicants clamoring for treatment. (Quoted in *Brattleboro Daily Reformer*)

"The troop compartments of the *Leviathan* were so crowded," Crosby notes:

> that the slightest inattention to daily cleaning would quickly turn them into impassable sties, especially with flu causing nosebleeds among 20 percent of the sick and seasickness causing vomiting among the sick and healthy. (132)

On the third morning at sea, when their officers ordered the men to clean the troop compartments below decks and carry out the sick and the dead, they refused (132). When a soldier disobeys a lawful order, it's called insubordination. Punishment can be as severe as time in jail with hard labor. When more than one soldier disobeys a lawful order, it's called mutiny and is punishable by death.

By that evening, October 2, a second victim succumbed to the flu. The next day, three more. Seven more the day after.

Then, from the ship's War Diary:

> [October 5] Total deaths to date, 21. Small force of embalmers impossible to keep up with rate of dying.
>
> [October 6] Total dead to date, 45. Impossible to embalm bodies fast enough. Signs of decomposing starting in some of them. (Quoted in Crosby, 133)

The medical officer's estimate puts the total flu cases during the voyage at 2,000 out of 12,000 aboard. Ninety of those died at sea.

October 7, the ship arrived at Brest. After disembarking, Private Clyde Potts marched, with those of the Fifty-Seventh who were able, through pouring rain to a muddy camp five miles away. On the march and at the camp, more men fell. Crosby counts upwards of 170 flu deaths from the division after the landing (134-135).

Clyde Brake escaped the Spanish flu. By the end of October, he was near Le Mans, where we lose his trail until September the next year.

According to *The US Army in WWI: Orders of Battle* (Rinaldi, 102), the Fifty-Seventh Pioneer was due to be converted to the 398th Infantry when the Armistice was signed. The East Tennessee Veterans Memorial Association website quotes a 1975 letter by a fellow September 5 draftee. Henry F. Forte writes that he was transferred from the Fifty-Seventh to the 329th Regiment, Eighty-Third Infantry Division, in the days prior to November 11. The Eighty-Third Division, in the Le Mans area at the time, was a "depot division," from which troops were rationed out to other units as replacements.

From Le Mans, we don't know where the army took Uncle Clyde. All we know is that "Potts, Clyde B." returned to the US, from Brest to Hoboken, aboard the *Agamemnon* one year later. In that time, he had been promoted to corporal and made a cook in the Army Service Corps.

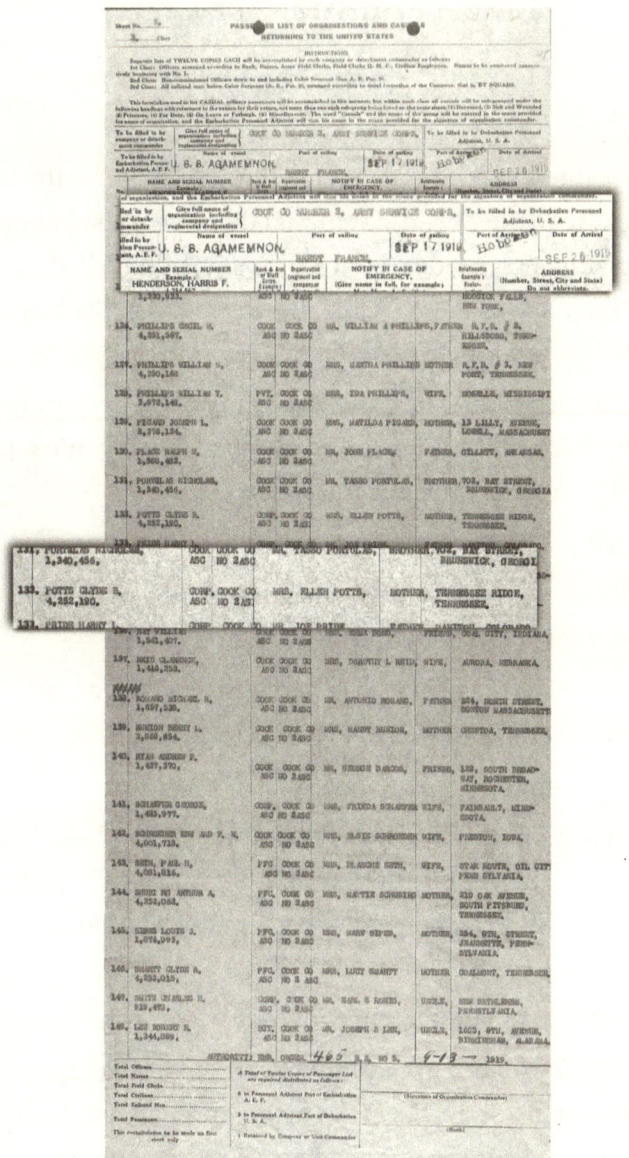

Clyde Brake Potts, the *Agamemnon*.
Back home, his brothers may have chided Clyde for being a cook, but their little brother outranked them.

26 Permission for Leave

OCTOBER 1918

In the Sommedieue Sector, Private B. F. Potts trudges along a roadside, head down, hands in pockets. He passes a group of his comrades from Company M huddled around a stool they use as a card table. Between turns, the boys laugh and talk about their upcoming leave.

Potts continues around the camp's soggy perimeter. A blaring horn that sounds like a goose careening into a puddle behind him interrupts his thoughts.

"Hey, Potts!"

He stops in the mud and turns. An ambulance driver hangs an arm out the window at him.

The driver speaks in a smooth Kansas accent. "Your brother's name's Roy, right?"

Potts nods.

"Well I just saw a Roy Potts at the 117th Field Hospital. He said he had a brother named Ben in the 137th. I reckon that's you, and I reckon your brother ain't as dead as you been told."

Tears leap to the corners of blue eyes. "Is he alright?"

"He was smokin' and jokin' this morning. After I drop these boys off here, I got to make another run back to the 117th. I'll be heading out in a few minutes if you want a ride."

"Don't leave without me!"

Potts dashes to division headquarters. The duty officer stands in the door, captain's bars on a collar. The private halts and assumes the position of attention. "Good afternoon, sir."

"Good afternoon, soldier. At ease." The captain is a slim man. Round-rimmed spectacles rest on a triangle nose. "Have we met before?"

"Didn't I see you in a shell hole during the withdraw in the Meuse, sir?"

"Yeah, I know you. Thanks for the heads up. We were so busy setting up the observation post, we didn't notice a whole battalion going back the other way!"

The captain laughs and introduces himself, offering a hand. Potts's ears perk up as he shakes the hand and gives his name.

"What can I do for you, Ben?"

"Well, sir . . ."

Ben had been told that Roy had died. Then he ran into someone who said, I just saw your brother over at so-and-so medical. So, he went to get a pass, and it was signed by Captain Harry S. Truman.

—John Potts

Twenty-seven years later, the man with the round-rimmed spectacles and triangle nose, who gave leave to Ben Potts to see his brother in a field hospital, who had commanded an artillery battery that fired countless high-explosive rounds upon the enemy in a small corner of France, would give the executive order that unleashed the most devastating weapon mankind has ever known.

27 An Unremarkable Day

OCTOBER 26, 1918

Nowhere in my research did I find that anything worth noting happened in the life of Benjamin Franklin Potts on this day a hundred years ago. He was in the Sommedieue sector in the trenches with the Thirty-Fifth Division. Haterius reports a few engagements during the week, involving other companies of the 137th Infantry Regiment, but Company M seems to have had an uneventful tour.

Between rotations in the trenches, the men read the international newspapers, where they learned that the Central Powers were showing signs of collapse. In previous weeks, Bulgaria had signed an armistice. The Ottoman Empire, without Bulgaria on its flank, was vulnerable to invasion, and ruler, Grand Vizier Talaat Pasha, had resigned with his entire ministry. The Imperial German Army was retreating before the Allied advance on the western front, and talk among the troops was of an end to the war, of peace, of going home.

October 26, 1918, is now significant only because fifty years later, one of Ben's granddaughters would add to his legacy of great grandsons. And fifty years after that, the great grandson would write that nothing worth noting happened in the life of his great grandfather a hundred years before.

We might guess that Private Potts on that day, like his sixth great grandson today, was thankful to have another day behind him, in which his life was not threatened, and another day before him, in which everything is possible.

28 Armistice, or A Railcar in the Woods

November 11, 1918

The wood is primeval. Prehistoric relics indicate human presence in the area of the Compiègne Forest since time immemorial. Beech, oak, and hornbeam trees sheltered game in Roman times. Since then, the forest has been the hunting ground of kings and emperors, the playground of princes and princesses, as well as a battleground. Julius Caesar fought the Gauls beneath its canopy. Merovingian kingdoms Austrasia and Neustria exchanged blows between its stout trunks.

During three days in November 1918, the ancient forest served as secret meeting place for negotiators of two warring sides seeking peace. A delegation for the German Empire arrived November 8. The Allied delegation was led by the supreme commander, French General Ferdinand Foch.

Negotiations took place in a railcar arranged for the purpose, positioned in a secluded glade near the French village of Rethondes, sixty miles north of Paris. General Foch chose the site to keep journalists at bay and avoid distractions.

Playing from a position of strength, Foch presented himself to members of the German delegation on the morning of the 8th, gave them a document listing the terms of a ceasefire, and told them they had seventy-two hours to sign it. He would return only once more.

The terms were strict: Withdrawal of all German forces back to prewar borders, plus evacuation of the Rhine Valley on Germany's western flank; surrender of all military equipment—artillery, machine guns, ships, aircraft, including trains and trucks; renunciation of two earlier treaties with Russia and Romania, and restoration of booty taken from those countries and Belgium. All infrastructure of evacuated territory was to remain intact, and the naval blockade of Germany would continue. The terms included no concessions by the Allies.

Hopeless as was their military position and with worsening social conditions at home, the Germans had no choice but to agree to the terms.

Between 5:12 and 5:20 a.m. on November 11, four members of the German delegation and a leading Allied representative signed the armistice. General Foch entered, examined the signatures, and, after adding his own mark to the document, departed for Paris. According to the conditions of the ceasefire, fighting would end within six hours.

With the 137th Regiment at Saint-Mihiel, Haterius recorded this scene in his journal. Private Benjamin Franklin Potts must have been within earshot. Through the journalist's words, we may relive the moment with our ancestor:

> At the eleventh hour on the eleventh day of the eleventh month, hostilities came to an end from Switzerland to the sea. Early that morning from the wireless station on the Eiffel Tower in Paris, there had gone forth through the air to the wondering, half-incredulous line the Americans held from near Sedan to the Moselle, the order from Marshal Foch to cease fire on the stroke of eleven.

On the stroke of eleven the cannon stopped, the rifles dropped from the shoulders, the machine guns grew still. There followed then a strange, unbelievable silence, as though the world had died. It lasted but a moment, lasted for the space that the breath is held. Then came such an uproar of relief and jubilance, such a tooting of horns, shrieking of whistles, such an overture from the bands and trains and church bells, such a shouting of voices as the earth is not likely to hear again in our day and generation. When night fell on the battlefield, the clamor of the celebration waxed rather than waned. Darkness? There was none. Rockets and a ceaseless fountain of starshells made the lines a streak of glorious brilliance across the face of startled France, while, by the light of flares, the Front and all its dancing, boasting, singing peoples was as clearly visible as though the sun sat high in the heavens. (181-182)

The ceasefire was prolonged three times before the final agreement, which included a clause that placed the blame for the war and all its ramifications on Germany. The intent was to prepare a legal case for war reparations, but when Germany signed the treaty on June 22, 1919, it humiliated the German people as well. Ratified on June 28, the Treaty of Versailles would bring the first of the world's two great wars to an end.

After a time in a museum at Les Invalides in Paris, the railcar in which the signing took place was moved back to the Compiègne Forest. The site became a historic monument and place of pilgrimage for tourists and survivors of veterans and war dead.

There, in the same secluded glade in the primeval forest, in the same railcar chosen by General Foch, another armistice would be signed twenty-two years after. June 22, 1940, Adolf Hitler chose the site for the formal surrender of France to Nazi Germany.

29 Cruel Days in Sampigny

WINTER 1918-19

With the ceasefire signed, the fighting was over, but the war wasn't ended. Though the possibility diminished as the enemy withdrew and gave up its arms, hostilities might recommence at any moment. The Allies' strong military position brought the Germans to Compiègne; continued pressure, in the form of a military occupation, would keep them at the negotiating table. Furthermore, the vanquished enemy's capacity to make war must be reduced.

He is not informed, nor does he care, about the greater military and political machinations. The soldier, once the job is done, turns his mind to home and family. Private Potts, with the 137th's Third Battalion, was billeted in Ménil-aux-Bois, a village outside Sampigny [*sam-peen-yee*] in the Saint-Mihiel area. There, he awaited orders and fought the soldier's fiercest enemy: boredom. Haterius calls it the "battle of Sampigny."

> We now entered upon what was to prove a long, cold, dark winter of training. [Camp] Doniphan days over again. Although the armistice had been signed and hostilities had ceased, it must be remembered that we were still in a state of war, and the enemy was engaged, but in a somewhat different manner. All units upon foreign soil must ever remain in a state of preparedness. Efficiency and co-operation were still the watchwords. All during the cold, wet winter months the boys underwent daily drill out on the rain-soaked fields and roads. Close order drills, field maneuvers, tactical

problems, simulated battles, rifle practice, and parades and inspections, constituted the curriculum. We were now resigned to the game of watchful waiting, and this proved far more unenduring than the game of war, so it seemed. It was a most disagreeable existence, and all in all, we hardly saw six days of sunshine during all the winter. (187)

Colonel Ira L. Reeves, who had taken command of the 137th Regiment in the Sommedieue trenches, is credited with the establishment of an athletics program to replace part of the daily drill. Colonel Reeves also consented to theatrical performances and organized a school, which offered lessons in English, French, and history to the regiment's officers and men. During this time, six issues of a regimental newspaper, *The Jayhawkerinfrance*, were printed on a local printing press. Thanksgiving and Christmas were observed with special menus and concerts by the regimental band.

A more devious foe in the battle of Sampigny was the rumor. One day, embarkation for the States was imminent. The next day, the division was to be part of the occupation army and march to Germany. Haterius writes: "Brutus, those were cruel days" (192).

30 Godspeed

FEBRUARY 17, 1919

It happened on Monday, February 17th, that the units of the 35th were called out and formed on a wide level stretch of the Meuse Valley near Commercy. Here twenty-two thousand men of the division passed in review of the Commander-in-Chief and the "petit" Prince of Wales, who was the guest of honor. (Haterius, 192)

Inspection by the Commander-in-Chief (US Army Signal Corps, 1919). General John J. Pershing (*center*) and Prince Edward of Wales (*middle left in visor cap*) inspect the troops of the Thirty-Fifth.

Twenty-four-year-old Prince Edward, who would become Edward VIII, King of England, made small impression on the men of the Thirty-Fifth. Ted Powell, in his book *King Edward VIII: An American Life*, writes:

> The doughboys [of the Thirty-Fifth] were in awe of "Black Jack" Pershing, leading the inspection with a group of senior officers on horseback, but were disappointed by the Prince of Wales. . . . The Prince went out of his way *not* to look like a "prince," for example refusing to wear the *Croix de Guerre* that the French had awarded him, on the grounds that he had done nothing to deserve it. (29)

In their *History* book, the men of Ambulance Company Number 139 (collective authors) are more specific about the parade ground location, placing it north of Commercy between the villages of Vignot and Boncourt-sur-Meuse. "The field itself, located on a broad stretch of the Meuse basin, was mush-like with mire and patched with pools of water" (73-74).

They describe the inspection and passing in review:

> The columns of the Division were drawn up into platoon fronts. . . . After riding around the Division, General Pershing and his party personally inspected each platoon, winding back and forth, asking questions of the company commanders and speaking with the men.
> Having completed the personal inspection, the General and his party took position in the reviewing stand on the right. At the command "Pass in Review" by the Division Commander, each battalion executed successively "Squads Right," and swept down the field

in a line of platoons. It was indeed a most impressive sight, and, although the sky was cast heavy with low-hanging clouds, the sun, as if to lend color to an already beautiful picture, broke through and shone for a few moments. Then, as each column swung out upon its own way home, the rain began again. . . .

Although participation in the great event required that the men wear full packs for almost nine hours without removing them, and undergo a hike of twenty kilos in the rain, not a man regretted the experience. It will be long remembered with pride by those who took part. (74)

Recognition from leaders is the soldier's reward. He risks life and limb and suffers daily hardships, not for pay, but for country: its values and its purpose. His recompense is the country's gratitude for duty done with honor. It marks the personal achievement, which each soldier, before it's met, wonders in his heart of hearts if he can accomplish.

For the troops, the AEF commander embodied the country. The commander's acknowledgment of a job well done set the laurel on their victory.

Later that day, in an address to officers, General Pershing announced the Thirty-Fifth's imminent departure and "wished the officers and men of the division Godspeed on their homeward journey" (Haterius, 193).

When Pershing visited, Grandpa was one of two men that put new shoes on his horse. When the general was ready to leave, Grandpa held the reins while he mounted.

—Bruce Potts

31 Easter Aboard the *Manchuria*

April 20, 1919

With orders for home, the 137th Regiment boarded trains at Sampigny on March 7. They arrived in the Le Mans area three days later. The companies were dispersed to surrounding towns and villages, Company M to Monfort-les-Gesnois. Far from the desolate battlefields, the men enjoyed a couple weeks of "the best accommodations since [their] arrival in France," whether in billets or private homes (Haterius, 197).

Following this respite, they moved to what was known as "the Belgian Camp," where they slept in tents and were subjected to medical examinations, inoculations, and "cootie baths" to make them presentable to their mothers.

April 4, an overnight train from Champagne took the regiment to the coast at Brest, France's westernmost port. After a week's wait in cantonment, a morning march, loaded with all their gear, took them to the docks. From there, they were conveyed by light boats to a transport ship anchored a mile out in the bay. France, as its final farewell, drizzled rain on them.

From the *Manchuria*'s passenger list, April 12, 1919. Although the "Date of Sailing" is recorded here as April 12, according to Haterius, the 137th boarded on the 11th, waited throughout the next day, and sailed on the 13th (205).

The *Manchuria* steamed out of the bay, setting course for Hoboken, New Jersey. Haterius describes the vessel:

> We were now on the good ship *Manchuria*, a former Pacific mail steamer which had plied between San Francisco and Hong Kong, China. This was her tenth voyage across the Atlantic. A brief description of her capacity: She had a length of 615 feet, displacement of 27,000 tons, took 1,056,000 gallons of fresh water, 40,000 tons of coal, sufficient for a round trip, two great engines, twelve boilers, thirty-six huge furnaces, and twin propellers. "Some baby" we agree. The compartments had all been taken out and bunks three high were crowded together, each section of three, two feet apart. It was somewhat crowded with 4,771 officers and enlisted men aboard. (202, 205)

The voyage was uneventful save for forty-foot waves on the sixth day, from which none were spared discomfort, and a holiday. On Sunday, April 20, the ship's chaplain held Easter services on board.

Thanks to the journal-keeping Haterius, we know what meal Private B. F. Potts shared with his comrades that Sunday a century ago: "For our Easter dinner, beans were served—nothing more, nothing less—beans and beans only" (206).

The following day the troops spotted the first seabirds flying overhead. Two days later, they set foot on native soil.

32 Homecoming

MAY 14, 1919

There were parades in that glorious spring of 1919. In New York and Washington, D.C., in small towns and state capitals, ranks of soldiers, formed in companies and led by the army band, marched down Main Streets across the United States. In Topeka, the officers and men of the 137th Infantry "All-Kansas" Regiment stepped with heads high, through cheering crowds, flags waving.

But Private Potts was not among his comrades of Company M. After disembarking the *Manchuria* at Hoboken, April 23, the Thirty-Fifth Division entrained to Camp Upton, New York. In the last week of April, all replacement soldiers, of which B. F. Potts was one, were detached from the division.

Private Potts was put on a southbound train to Fort Oglethorpe, Georgia, where he was discharged May 12. He was given train fare for home and remaining pay, plus a sixty-dollar bonus.

In a small town in Middle Tennessee, Jack and Ellen Potts stand on a platform beside the tracks. Susie, at twenty their youngest child and only daughter, is there. As is their eldest, William Rufus, with his wife Annie and their children. Ruby and Jack run about, shoes clomping on wooden planks. Annie holds fifteen-month-old Bertha. Roy Albert, who came home the month before, now awaits his brother. Jack and Ellen's youngest boy, Clyde Brake, would return in September.

A slim young man in uniform, overseas cap cocked on his head, steps from the train as it screeches to a stop. He is clean-shaven and smiling, ears perked. The steam whistle announces a hero's arrival, a son's return.

Two years later, October 8, 1921, Benjamin Franklin Potts married Lucinda Mae Tanner. They had four children: daughters Viola Francis, called "Nanna" by her grandchildren, Imogene Brownie, who died at age three from scarlet fever, and twin boys Jesse Calvin and John Wesley. Ben and Mae's descendants number thirteen grandchildren and thirty-six great grandchildren, plus fifty-eight two- and three-times great grandchildren to date.

In following years, Ben moved the family several times between Tennessee and Michigan for work. In Tennessee, he worked for the L&N Railroad, most notably as a detonation man, making way for new track with dynamite. In Detroit, he worked for Cadillac, from which he retired in 1962.

In 1942, at age forty-seven, Ben Potts registered for the draft the second time in his life.

Grandpa Ben wanted to go fight in WWII and registered, but they wouldn't take him.

—Bruce Potts

Following retirement, with the children grown, Ben and Mae moved back to their hometown, Tennessee Ridge, Tennessee, where they lived in a red brick house. They tended a vegetable garden in the back yard and kept chickens in a coop. Ben drove Mae to church every Sunday. They had frequent family visits.

After Sunday dinner, the family moves out to the carport, shaded from the summer sun. Children, grandchildren, and their children sit in lawn chairs, sipping Granny's iced tea from plastic cups. Grandpa Ben hangs his cane on the chair's arm and cuts a plug of tobacco with a pocketknife. A breeze blows from the rose garden, and Nanna asks:

"Well, Daddy, what did you think about France?"

Ben and Mae Potts, 1942.

Grandpa brought his dented helmet home to Tennessee Ridge. Granny used it as a water bowl for the chickens until it rusted out.

—*Bruce Potts*

Appendix I Discharge and Enlistment Record

Included here are Benjamin F. Potts's discharge and enlistment record, two sides of the same paper, accompanied by a transcript, including that of stamps and a pencil mark on the latter.

Based on the penmanship (in which I am no expert), the lieutenant, signatory of the enlistment record, seems to be the scribe.

In the transcript, handwritten text is shown in italics. Where the original is illegible, I have compared with other handwritten text in the document and with similar records to derive a probable text, which I enclose in brackets. Where this is impossible, I leave an ellipsis between brackets.

Asterisks (*), daggers (†), and double daggers (‡) indicate footnotes on either side of the form, also transcribed. Superscript numbers mark my own notes.

The following information about the form is given in the footer margins:

Form No. 525. A. G. O.[1]
Oct. 9-18.
3—3164

---

[1] Adjutant General's Office.

Appendix I

Honorable Discharge from The United States Army
TO ALL WHOM [IT] MAY CONCERN:

This is to Certify, [That* *Benjamin F. Potts*]

† *3501865*[2] *Private Co "M" 137th Infantry*

THE UNITED STATES ARMY, as a Testimonial of Honest and Faithful Service, is hereby Honorably Discharged from the military service of the United States by reason of‡ *Exp. Of Ser. Per Cir. 106 W. D. 12/3/18*[3]

Said *Benjamin F. Potts* was born in *Slayden*, in the State of *Tennessee* When enlisted he was 23 9/12 years of age and by occupation a *R. R. Foreman*[4]

He had *Blue* eyes, *D. Brown* hair, *Fair* complexion, and was 5 feet 3 1/4 inches in height.

Given under my hand at *Fort Oglethorpe Ga* this *12th* day of *May*, one thousand nine hundred and *nineteen*

[G. H. Blankenship][5]
Major 46th Infantry
Commanding.
U. S. A.

* Insert name, Christian name first: e.g., "John Doe."

† Insert Army serial number, grade, company and regiment or arm or corps or department, e.g., "1,620,302"; "Corporal, Company A, 1st Infantry"; "Sergeant, Quartermaster Corps"; "Sergeant, First Class, Medical Department."

‡ If discharged prior to expiration of service, give number, date, and source of order or full description of authority therefor.

---

[2] The numeral 1 here could be a 7. Other documents, like the *Tunisian's* passenger list (page 17), show a 1.

[3] Expiration of Service per Circular 106 War Department, December 3, 1918. Circular 106 stipulates that a soldier must be discharged from the army post closest to home.

[4] During his service, B. F. Potts was not promoted in military rank. He was, however, promoted from railroad trackman at induction (page 11) to foreman.

[5] I made out some letters and guessed the rest. An internet search reveals a Major G. H. Blankenship of the 46th Infantry signed other discharges at Fort Oglethorpe.

Honorable Discharge from The United States Army

TO ALL WHOM IT MAY CONCERN:

This is to Certify _that_ _____
1,950,865 Private Co. _13th Infantry_

THE UNITED STATES ARMY, as a Testimonial of Honest and Faithful Service, is hereby Honorably Discharged from the military service of the United States by reason of _Cyp of Ser. per Cir. 106 W.D. 13/9_

Said _Benjamin S. Potts_ was born in _Clayborn_, in the State of _Tennessee_. When enlisted he was _32_ years of age, and by occupation a _R.R. Foreman_. He had _Blue_ eyes, _D.B._ hair, _Fair_ complexion, and was _5_ feet _3 1/4_ inches in height.

Given under my hand at _Fort Oglethorpe Ga._ this _12th_ day of _May_, one thousand nine hundred and _Nineteen_.

Major 46th Infantry
Commanding
U.S.A.

Form No. 525, A. G. O.
Oct. 9-18.

ENLISTMENT RECORD.

Name: Benjamin J Pate Grade: Private
Enlisted, or Inducted: June 28, 1918 at Crew, Tennessee
Serving in: first _____ enlistment period at date of discharge.
Prior service:* None

Noncommissioned officer: No
Marksmanship: Not qualified

Battles, engagements, skirmishes, expeditions: Meuse Argonne, Lost Scout Bouce Defense Sector - Nov 6, 1918
Decorations, Medals, Badges, Citations: None
Knowledge of any vocation: Coal Mine Foreman
Wounds received in service: None
Physical condition when discharged: Good
Typhoid prophylaxis completed: Aug 1918
Paratyphoid prophylaxis completed: Aug 1918
Married or single: Single
Character: Excellent

Ho. M.P. Ord. _____ 1918
Soldier entitled to travel pay to Crew, Tenn.
Served with the A.E.F. from Aug 23, 1918 till April 23, 1919

Signature of soldier: Benjamin J Pate

WC Thurman
1st Lt 46th Infantry
Commanding Casual Det.

ENLISTMENT RECORD.

Name: *Benjamin F. Potts* Grade: *Private*
Enlisted, or Inducted, *June 28, 1918*, at *Erin, Tennessee*
Serving in *First* enlistment period at date of discharge.
Prior service: * *None*
Noncommissioned officer: [*Never*]
[Marksmanship, gunner qualification or rating: † *None of record*]
Horsemanship: [*Not mounted*]
Battles, engagements, skirmishes, expeditions: *Sommedieue Sub-Sector Bouée Defense Oct. 14 - Nov. 6, 1918*[6]
Decorations, Medals, Badges, Citations; None
Knowledge of any vocation: *Rail Road Foreman*
Wounds received in service: *None*
Physical condition when discharged: *Normal*
Typhoid prophylaxis completed: *Aug. [. . .] 1918*
Paratyphoid prophylaxis completed: *Aug. [. . .] 1918*
Married or single: *Single*
Character: *Excellent*[7]
[Remarks:] *No A. W. O. L. [under] G. O. 31/12 or 45/14*[8]
Soldier entitled to travel pay to Erin, Tenn.[9]
Served with the A. E. F. from Aug. 23, 1918 till April 23, 1919
Signature of soldier: *Benjamin F. Potts*

> [W. C.] *Thurman*
> 1st Lt 46th *Infantry*
> Commanding *Casual Det*[10]

* Give company and regiment or department, with inclusive dates of service in each enlistment.
† Give date of qualification or rating and number, date, and source of order announcing same.

---

[6] See Appendix II.

[7] Other discharge papers imply the US Army honorably discharged only persons of "excellent" character.

[8] No Absence Without Leave under General Orders No. 31, War Department, 1912, or No. 45, War Department, 1914.

[9] The army paid five cents per mile. (See note 13.)

[10] Casual Detachment. A "casual" is a soldier not assigned to a unit.

In the upper- and lower-left corners of the enlistment record are faded stamps, in purple, red, and blue, and a penciled number. The red one may be three stamps, separated in the transcript by dashes.

(Purple ink, in rectangle)
[FORWA]RDED: NOV 1[5 1920]
[APPRO]VED: E. G. Cow[en]
FOR VICTO[RY MEDAL][11] WITH   (Red ink)
DEFENSIVE SECTOR[12]   PAID IN FULL *89.05*[13]
      INCLUDING $60 BONUS
      [PRO]VIDED IN SEC 140[6 REVENUE ACT]
      OF 1918 APPROVED [FEB 24TH]
      1919.[14] FT OGLETHORPE
      —
      MAY 12 1919
(Blue ink, curved)   —
TICKET OFFICE   GEO. [H. CHASE]
MAY 13 19   CAPT [Q. M. C.][16]
CHATTANOOGA[15]   FINANCE [OFFICER]

---

[11] As per General Order No. 48, 1919, US Army soldiers who served honorably between April 6, 1917, and November 11, 1918, qualified for the Victory Medal, a bronze disk with a winged Victory on the front.

[12] Participation in thirteen major battles of WWI, including the Meuse-Argonne Offensive, was recognized with a clasp. The Defensive Sector clasp represented participation in any other battle or service in the trenches.

[13] This, in pencil, is a dollar amount. A private earned $30 a month. A prorated portion, $12, plus the bonus, from $89.05 leaves $17.05 in travel pay. (See note 9.) This implies a distance of 341 miles, which corresponds to the route from Chattanooga through Stevenson, AL, and Nashville, TN, to McKenzie on the Nashville, Chattanooga & St. Louis Railway, then to Erin on the Louisville & Nashville RR (Poor, *Manual of Railroads*, map facing 82).

[14] Within days of the Armistice, the US Congress adopted Section 1406 as an amendment to the year's revenue act, which was approved in 1919.

[15] Boarding the train at Chattanooga's Terminal Station, outside Fort Oglethorpe, Ben Potts was already in his home state.

[16] Quarter Master Corps.

Appendix II   Alternative Scenario

The narrative outlines a possible itinerary for B. F. Potts's journey. But what if I've got it all wrong?

The enlistment record shows Benjamin F. Potts in the Sommedieue sector from October 14 to November 6. It does not show the Meuse-Argonne.

An administrative oversight? Suppose, for whatever reason, the lieutenant-scribe didn't have the proper documents for Potts's participation in the Argonne battle. The soldier on his way home, already putting the war behind him, may not care enough to insist. Even if he did, without the document any argument would lack conviction.

Or, is it possible that Private Potts left the States on August 24 and didn't join the Thirty-Fifth Division until mid-October? The following anecdote from Haterius suggests it is.

Amid the Armistice celebrations, a truck pulled up to the front, writes Haterius:

> Over the tailboard ... there gazed a boy who had been drafted in the heart of America some six months before, and who with stopoffs for tedious training on the way, had slowly journeyed from his home to the Ardennes. (184-185)

Furthermore, Haterius mentions the reception of "a large number of replacements" after the Argonne battle, on the 11th of October, at a camp between the villages Benoîte Vaux and Récourt-le-Creux. "These men hailed from Camp Gordon.

They were natives of the States of Kentucky, Tennessee, Georgia, Alabama and Mississippi" (172).

That Haterius or any other chronicler doesn't mention receiving replacements after coming out of the Vosges ("Rendezvous with the Thirty-Fifth Division") is not surprising. The hundred men replaced among the twenty-seven-thousand strong division would be hardly notable.

In any case, an alternative scenario is that B. F. Potts, after landing at a French port in early September ("Rendezvous"), spent a month in a depot division, as did Clyde Brake ("Nightmare at Sea"), before joining his unit on October 11.

Considering Grandpa Ben's war stories, three concern the period in question:

1. Entrained soldiers, stopped for the night on the tracks, might have burgled the bakery ("Rendezvous") during the ride to the supposed depot division or from it to the rendezvous with the Thirty-Fifth.

2. The nighttime bombardment of an empty building ("A Potts Family Day of Thanks") could have happened during the march into the Sommedieue sector. None of our journalists, however, mention any bombing on the way, including Haterius who goes into some detail about the movement. Of the night of October 11, he writes: "We commenced hearing the distant detonations of guns and saw occasional flashes off to the east and north" (172). This seems an opportunity to include a nearby bombing if such had occurred.

3. Lastly, "Encounter at Creek's Edge" hints at Grandpa Ben's presence in the Argonne battle. The scenario seems

unlikely in the Sommedieue trenches, where the battle lines are firm. Neither soldier would wander across no-man's-land—not alone, and not in daylight.

The reader may draw his or her own conclusions.

Appendix III   The Truman Encounters

As stated in the preface to this volume, scenes told in present tense are fictional. Three such scenes recount Private Potts's encounters with an artillery officer, who gives him permission for leave in the final meeting. In the first, the officer helps to pull a gun through the mud. In the second, we recognize the same officer setting up an observation post in a shell hole, not noticing that the troops are withdrawing.

While, again, the encounters are fictional, the first and second are drawn from actual events. Future US President Harry Truman served in the Missouri National Guard's Second Field Artillery Regiment as an enlisted man from 1905 to 1911. In 1917, as a first lieutenant, he rejoined the regiment, which was later federalized, becoming the 129th Regiment in the Sixtieth Field Artillery Brigade, Thirty-Fifth Infantry Division. Promoted to captain in July 1918, Truman was assigned command of the 129th's Battery D.

D. M. Giangreco, former editor of the US Army's *Military Review* and author of two biographical books on the former president, studied Truman's handwritten notes, extensive oral histories of the soldiers who served under his command, and records of other commanders in the 129th. He collated this information with battalion and division orders to derive a detailed timetable of the captain's movements during the Argonne battle. Giangreco published his findings in the *Journal of the Royal Artillery* ("Truman in the Argonne," 56-59).

The initial encounter takes place September 26, the battle's first day. Of the afternoon, Giangreco writes:

Truman and his battery then followed the rest of his regiment across no-man's-land and was often forced to pull his guns one at a time by double teaming—that's 12 horses—in order to get them through the muddy, shell-torn German minefields.

Although the second encounter takes place on the battle's fourth day in this narrative, Giangreco puts Truman in the precarious position on the second day, September 27:

> Truman was again sent forward to observe and direct fire in support of the assault on Charpentry....
> Unnoticed, however, some "shifting and straightening" of the U.S. infantry's lines had begun. The result? Truman's shell-crater OP ended up ... some 200 yards in advance of the regiment it was to support. So intent had he and his small group been at observing fire and setting up wire communications, that they hadn't recognized the full-blown pullback in the smoke and confusion, and disaster was prevented by one of the last infantrymen out who warned them of the move.

Private Potts's third encounter with the artillery officer is based solely on Grandpa's anecdote.

Annotated Bibliography

The following is a list of selected sources used in research for this book. I give notes on those I found most useful.

For the reader who would like more details about what life was like for B. F. Potts and about his movements with the 137th Regiment, I draw attention to the works of three authors: Haterius, Hoyt, and Kenamore, who were with the regiment or its parent division.

Where a source is available on the World Wide Web, I give a URL. All web addresses below were last accessed March 15, 2019.

American Battle Monuments Commission. *30th Division, Summary of Operations in the World War*. Washington, DC: United States Government Printing Office, 1944. https://babel.hathitrust.org/cgi/pt?id=uc1.b3110102.

To accompany this and similar volumes, including one for the Thirty-Fifth Division (below), the ABMC also produced maps showing each division's position during the battles in which it participated. For high-resolution digital versions of the ABMC maps used in this book, see the web page: https://www.stephenwendell.com/avmp/.

American Battle Monuments Commission. *35th Division, Summary of Operations in the World War*. Washington, DC: United States Government Printing Office, 1944. https://babel.hathitrust.org/cgi/pt?id=uc1.b3110105.

American Battle Monuments Commission. *American Armies and Battlefields in Europe: A History, Guide, and Reference Book.* Washington, DC: United States Government Printing Office, 1938.
https://www.abmc.gov/sites/default/files/publications/AABEFINAL_Blue_Book.pdf.

Ambulance Company Number 139. *History of Ambulance Company Number 139.* Kansas City, KS: E. R. Callender, n.d.
https://archive.org/details/historyofambulan00kansiala/.

Association of the Friends of Vauquois and its Region. "Mound of Vauquois." http://butte-vauquois.fr/en/.

The website of the Association of the Friends of Vauquois and its Region has photos and information on visiting the site. The guided tour of the underground galleries, where the mine war took place, is enlightening, educational, and horrific.

Crosby, Alfred W. *America's Forgotten Pandemic: The Influenza of 1918.* New York: Cambridge University Press, 2003.

East Tennessee Veterans Memorial Association (website). "Arl B. Kelly."
https://etvma.org/veterans/arl-b-kelly-6676/.

Giangreco, D. M. "Captain Harry Truman and Battery D, 129th Field Artillery, in Action in the Argonne." *Journal of the Royal Artillery* 130, no. 3 (Autumn 2003): 56-59.

Giangreco is the author of several books on military and sociopolitical topics, including two about Harry Truman: *Dear Harry . . . : Truman's Mailroom, 1945-1953* (Stackpole Books, 1999) and *The Soldier from Independence: A Military Biography of Harry Truman* (Zenith, 2009). The journal article is also found at Worldwar1.com's Doughboy Center: http://www.worldwar1.com/dbc/truman2.htm.

Haterius, Carl E. *Reminiscences of the 137th U. S. Infantry.* Topeka, KS: Crane, 1919. https://archive.org/details/reminiscencesof100hate/.

Haterius was a band member in the 137th who kept a diary. Although events sometimes run together and the dates can be nebulous, what Haterius does well is give the ambiance—what it felt like at a place and time. He also reproduces the division and brigade orders for the beginning of the Meuse-Argonne Offensive.

Hoyt, Charles B. *Heroes of the Argonne: An Authentic History of the Thirty-Fifth Division.* Compiled by C. B. Lyon, Jr. Kansas City, MO: Franklin Hudson, 1919. https://archive.org/details/heroesofargonnea00hoyt/.

A private first class in the 139th Field Hospital, Hoyt wrote this history from official records, orders, and interviews with officers and men of the division. While it lacks Haterius's intimacy and Kenamore's detail, the book corroborates dates and places, and accompanying the text are plentiful maps and photographs.

Hurley, Edward N. *The Bridge to France*. Philadelphia, PA: J. B. Lippincott, 1927.
http://www.gwpda.org/wwi-www/Hurley/.

Kenamore, Clair. *From Vauquois Hill to Exermont: A History of the Thirty-Fifth Division of the United States Army*. St. Louis, MO: Guard, 1919.
https://archive.org/details/fromvauquoishill00ken/.

Kenamore had previously reported on another of General John J. Pershing's exploits, the Mexican Expedition, in 1916. When the officers and men of the Missouri and Kansas National Guard units shipped to Europe, Kenamore followed. A correspondent for the *St. Louis Post-Dispatch*, he reported back to the folks at home the activities of their sons on the front. After the war, he collected articles and notes to write this history of the Thirty-Fifth Division.

King, Benjamin, Richard C. Biggs, and Eric R. Criner. *Spearhead of Logistics: A History of the United States Army Transportation Corps*. Washington, DC: Center of Military History, 2001.

Poor, Henry V. *Poor's Manual of Railroads: Fifty-Third Annual Number*. New York: Poor's, 1920.
https://babel.hathitrust.org/cgi/pt?id=uc1.a0002685253.

Powell, Ted. *King Edward VIII: An American Life*. Oxford: Oxford University Press, 2018.

Rinaldi, Richard A. *The United States Army in World War I: Orders of Battle, Ground Units, 1917-1919*. Takoma Park, MD: General Data, 2005.

Smith, Eugene W. *Trans-Atlantic Passenger Ships Past and Present*. Boston, MA: George H. Dean, 1947. https://archive.org/details/transatlanticpas00smitrich/.

Stuart, Richard W., ed. *American Military History Volume II: The United States Army in a Global Era, 1917-2008*. Washington, DC: Center of Military History, 2010. https://www.armyupress.army.mil/Portals/7/educational-services/military-history/american-military-history-volume-2.pdf.

> The US Army's Center for Military History produced this thorough but brief text, which covers the nation's military history up to Afghanistan and Iraq in two volumes. Volume II, Chapter 1: "The U.S. Army in World War I, 1917–1918," covers our target period in fifty pages, including maps, photos, and informative sidebars.

Sparks, Winnie, ed. *Livingston County Illinois in the World War*. N.p.: Board of Supervisors of Livingston County, n.d.

www.ingramcontent.com/pod-product-compliance
Lightning Source LLC
LaVergne TN
LVHW041813060526
838201LV00046B/1250